Poetry
Book Society

THE FIRST
TWENTY-FIVE
YEARS

edited by
Eric W. White
for members of
the Society

LONDON
Poetry Book Society
1979

Acknowledgments

All contributions are reprinted by permission of the authors concerned. Thanks are also due to A. D. Peters & Co Ltd for the Edmund Blunden contribution, to R. Dardis Clarke for Austin Clarke, to Professor Christopher Cornford for Frances Cornford, to Valerie Eliot for T. S. Eliot, to Patrick Hamilton for George Rostrevor Hamilton, to Mollie Elkin and Trustees for David Jones, to Professor E. R. Dodds for Louis MacNeice, to Gavin Muir for Edwin Muir, to Rupert Hart-Davis for William Plomer, to Beatrice Roethke Lushington for Theodore Roethke, and to Gwen Watkins for Vernon Watkins.

No book of W. H. Auden's was ever submitted to the Society for choice or recommendation; but he was closely associated with the Society's festivals where he made frequent appearances as a reader of his poems. In 1972 he became a member of the Board of Management, about a year before his death. To commemorate his interest in the Society and its activities, it seemed appropriate here to reprint his poem 'On the Circuit', even though it refers to readings in other places and another continent. The manuscript reproduced is a fair copy which he wrote in May 1964 in a blank book belonging to Eric W. White. It appears here by courtesy of Edward Mendelson.

Introduction

THE ARTS COUNCIL AND LITERATURE

When in 1945 the Arts Council of Great Britain cast off its wartime CEMA chrysalis, it had established current policies for helping drama, opera and ballet, music, and the visual arts, but nothing for literature. In fact, some people like A.P. Herbert went so far as to maintain that the wording of the aims and objects clause in the Royal Charter expressly excluded literature from its scope. This was not so; but shortage of cash certainly made the Council understandably nervous about taking on new commitments.

In 1949 the Government invited the Arts Council to assume responsibility for the arts side of the Festival of Britain 1951; and the Council began to consider the possibility of launching a number of commission schemes. It was speedily agreed that commissions should be placed with painters, sculptors and composers; but it seemed unjust that nothing should be done for poets as well. So the Council invited a small group of writers – Richard Church, C. Day-Lewis, Sir George Rostrevor Hamilton, Christopher Hassall, and L. A. G. Strong – to put up suggestions, and on their advice a world-wide competition was launched for poetry written in English. In the event, the prize-winning poems were published as a Penguin under the title *Poems 1951*, edited by John Hayward.

From the beginning this group of five writers made it clear they did not rate very high the value of a competition in encouraging poets and poetry, and they urged the Council to show evidence of its serious intent by adopting a continuing policy of help to poetry and setting aside part of its annual grant-in-aid for this purpose. Their arguments bore fruit, and the Council agreed to appoint a panel to advise it on poetry policy. The original membership consisted of the five writers already mentioned, with Joseph Compton, a member of the Council, as Chairman.

CREATION OF THE POETRY BOOK SOCIETY

Early in the 1950s, Stephen Spender mooted the idea of a 'poetry book club' as deserving support. There was publicity in *Picture Post*, as a result of which several hundred letters were received from members of the public. Victor Gollancz was informally consulted and made some suggestions about the finances of such a club. At this point, the Arts Council on the advice of its Poetry Panel, agreed to convene a meeting of representatives of various publishing houses in order to try to assess their reactions to the idea. The following were invited to a meeting early in 1953, at which Joseph Compton took the chair:—

D. M. Cohen	(Cresset Press)
T. S. Eliot	(Faber & Faber)
John Lehmann	(John Lehmann)
C. Day Lewis	(Chatto & Windus)
Robert Lusty	(Michael Joseph)
Erica Marx	(Hand & Flower Press)
John Murray	(John Murray)
Ian Parsons	(Chatto & Windus)
Herbert Read	(Routledge & Kegan Paul)

By April 1953, detailed proposals were ready for submission to the Arts Council, which agreed that an independent Poetry Book Society should be set up as a company limited by guarantee and not having a share capital. At this stage it was thought that a launching grant of about £2,000 would be needed; and this money was found by drawing £1,000 from the current Poetry Panel allocation together with a further £1,000 from a special projects allocation earmarked for the Arts Council Regional Offices. A meeting at which the Poetry Book Society Ltd was formally constituted was held on 3 December 1953.

The first directors were:—

B. H. Blackwell	T. S. Eliot
Joseph Compton	Sir George Rostrevor Hamilton
R. N. David	Erica Marx

Joseph Compton was elected Chairman of the Board, and Eric W. White, the Assistant Secretary of the Arts Council, was appointed the company's first secretary. The intention was that the new organisation should be housed in the National Book League; but after a brief trial period it was discovered that this did not work satisfactorily, and it was decided to revert to the original arrangement whereby the Arts Council offered the Society accommodation in its offices. When Eric W. White retired from the Arts Council in 1971, his place as Secretary of the Society was taken by Charles Osborne, the Council's new Literature Director.

The Society's main terms of reference, as set out in its articles and memorandum of association, are 'to further the education of the people of this country by fostering and propagating the art of poetry and particularly by promoting knowledge, appreciation and enjoyment of the published work of contemporary poets, and to formulate, prepare and establish schemes therefor, provided that all objects of the Society shall be of a charitable nature'. Since its inauguration the Society has offered its members a service consisting of four new books of poetry a year. Books already accepted for publication are submitted by their publishers in proof form prior to publication. These are read by specially appointed selectors, who are changed from year to year. This service is undoubtedly of special benefit to those who live in isolated parts of the country, or overseas, and find it difficult to be in touch with a good bookseller. Over the years the Society's subscribing membership has varied between 700 and over 1000; and it is estimated that in the quarter century of its existence (1954-1978) it has distributed nearly 100,000 volumes of new poetry to its members. These are not startling figures, but assured sales of this order are of real benefit to poets and publishers in the present-day economics of publishing. An annual subvention is received from the Arts Council.

THE BULLETIN AND OTHER PUBLICATIONS

With each choice, the Society distributes to members a Bulletin, which carries a special contribution by the poet of the choice and also particulars of any recommendations made by the selectors. In the period under review there have been ninety-nine choices and one-hundred and twenty-three recommendations. Some of the contributions written by the poets concerned are of more than ephemeral interest; and I have gathered together about forty items here – a personal choice – which I think are well worth rereading. These include some special items such as obituaries, and in the case of T. S. Eliot part of an address on Poetry and the Schools that he delivered at a press conference convened by the Poetry Book Society in 1956.

On The Circuit

Among pelagian travellers,
Lost on their lewd conceited way
To Massachusetts, Michigan,
Miami or L.A.,

An airborne instrument, I sit,
Predestined nightly to fulfill
Columbia Giesen Management's
Unfathomable will,

By whose election justified,
I bring my gospel of the Muse
To fundamentalists, to nuns,
To gentiles and to Jews,

And daily, seven days a week,
Before a local sense has jelled,
From talking-site to talking-site
Am jet-or-prop-propelled,

Though warm my welcome everywhere.
I shift so frequently, so fast,
I cannot now say where I was
The evening before last,

Unless some singular event
Should intervene to save the place
A truly asinine remark,
A soul-bewitching face,

Or blessed encounter, full of joy,
Unscheduled on the Giesen Plan,
With here, an addict of Tolkien,
There, a Charles Williams fan.

Since Merback lit a dunghill is,
I mount the rostrum unafraid
Indeed, 'twere damnable to ask
If I am overpaid.

Spirit is willing to repeat
Without a qualm the same old talk
But Flesh is homesick for our snug
Apartment in New York.

A sulky fifty-six, he finds
A change in meal-time utter hell,
Grown far too crochety to like
A luxury hotel

The Bible is a goodly book
I always can peruse with zeal
But really cannot say the same
For Hilton's __Be My Guest__,

Nor bear with equanimity
The radio in students' cars,
Musak at breakfast, or—dear God!—
Girl organists in bars

Then worst of all, the anxious thought,
Each time my plane begins to
And the No Smoking sign comes
__What will there be to drink?__

__Is this a milieu where I must
How grahamgreeneish! How infra dig!
Snatch from the bottle in my bag
An analeptic swig?__

W.H.A.

And the morning comes: I see,
... king below me on the plain,
The roofs of our more ancient
I shall not see again.

God bless the lot of them, although
I don't remember which were which;
God bless the USA, so large,
So friendly, and so rich

W. H. Auden

From almost its first issue, the Bulletin has also carried poems as 'fill-ins', usually by the poet of the recommendation (if any) in order to give readers a taste of his wares. From 1957 it became customary also to invite a poet to compile a Poetry Supplement for Christmas. In this way the Society has published a rich haul of new poems over the years. Each Poetry Supplement naturally reflects the taste of its editor; and I have resisted the temptation to make a new anthology here by cannibalising other editors' work. Instead, I have reprinted a poem Roy Fuller wrote following a press reception in 1974 on the occasion of the Poetry Book Society's twentieth anniversary. It appeared in the Bulletin for Summer 1974 and was reprinted in his collection *From the Joke Shop*, which was a recommendation in 1975. The poet enlarged it for the present occasion. And I have included David Jones's *A, a, a, Domine Deus* which appeared in the 1966 Christmas Poetry Supplement. I do so to commemorate the fact that, so far as I know, this was the first occasion on which this fragment appeared in its definitive text and correct lay-out. An imperfect version had been used for its first appearance in *Epoch and Artist*, Faber 1959. The correct version, as it appears in the Poetry Book Society Bulletin, was reprinted later in the special David Jones issue of *Agenda*, Spring-Summer 1967, and in *The Sleeping Lord*, Faber 1974.

9

FESTIVALS

Before the war John Masefield had started a verse-speaking festival in Oxford – a kind of non-competitive festival, with classes for verse speaking and adjudication, and occasional lectures and recitals. After the war it migrated to London, where it became known as the English Festival of Spoken Poetry. In the course of time its London organisers began to feel the need for a different type of festival, where poetry could be presented on a professional basis in its own right; and it was thought that the business of verse-speaking could be left to the care of bodies like the Poetry Society and the various schools of drama. The Poetry Book Society was approached and in 1961, with the support of the Arts Council, decided to mount what proved to be the first of a series of festivals of poetry. The Mermaid Theatre was taken for a week; John Wain appointed director; and the programme featured poetry readings in English and other languages, commissioned poems, recorded poetry, folk poetry, poetic drama, and films, lectures and discussions on subjects connected with poetry.

'Poetry at the Mermaid' captured the public's imagination; and the Poetry Book Society felt sufficiently encouraged to adopt a biennial festival pattern for the immediate future. The next two festivals were held at the Royal Court Theatre, with Patric Dickinson as director in 1963 and Douglas Cleverdon as Director in 1965. By then it was felt that there were serious disadvantages in presenting poetry within the framework of a theatre, particularly where a proscenium arch provided a sharp separation between reader and auditor; and it was decided that the 1967 festival (directors: Patrick Garland and Ted Hughes) should be held in the newly opened Queen Elizabeth Hall and Purcell Room on the South Bank. At the same time the scope of the festival was widened by throwing it open to poets from overseas, which meant not only English-speaking poets from the Commonwealth and the United States, but also poets speaking foreign tongues that would need translation. The first 'Poetry International' (as it was christened) was a sell-out, thanks partly to the appearance of enormously popular figures such as W. H. Auden, Allen Ginsberg, and Pablo Neruda. After the 1969 'Poetry International' the festival became an annual fixture, with its direction in the hands of Patrick Garland and Charles Osborne. The main recitals have usually been held in the Queen Elizabeth Hall, with less formal programmes and discussions taking place in the Institute of Contemporary Arts.

Eric W. White

Selected Contributions to the Society's Bulletin and Other Publications Reprinted

Spring 1954   The Death Bell: Poems and Ballads

I prefer my poems to speak for themselves, but I have been asked to supply a note about the poems and also about my method of composition.

I began writing when I was very young. I collected the English poets one by one, starting at the age of seven. My imagination was stirred by lyric poetry more than by any other kind of reading. Twenty years later I became aware that writers of poetry are of two kinds, those who write to an instrument and those who neglect the instrument for the sake of action, leaving it, as it were in the next room. My own poems all belong to the first category. I believe that the freedom offered to a lyric poet is not offered on easy terms; he must refuse rhetoric, and be attentive to the possibility of freedom within the restraint of the poem, a freedom much greater and more rewarding to the imagination than any other. The poet who makes fifty drafts for the sake of one knows this, and he understands that the poet who neglects the instrument has chosen an easier freedom because he has not the patience or perseverance to listen. Poetry is the interest of many, but the vocation of very few.

I have been told that the occasional expositions of my poems which I have read on the air are more obscure than the poems themselves, and perhaps this is inevitable. A poet is able to throw light on the source of a poem, but he cannot simplify it; he can only make it more difficult. The true simplicity of a good poem is always intricate and difficult, and the false simplicity of a prose paraphrase is bound to render it inaccessible. The most one can do is to state the theme.

Perhaps I should go no further until I have quoted an example. Here is a note I made stating the theme of one of the poems in this book, 'Egyptian Burial, Resurrection in Wales': 'In ancient Egypt the mummified body of a queen was commonly swathed in masterpieces of art written upon papyrus. Wine-vessels, money, and ears of corn were laid close at hand as they would be needed on the soul's journey. These were for sustenance and the manuscript for protection. The mummy and the tomb were themselves works of art in which every detail was important. The rarefied nature of the dead would carry with it all that was richest and purest in life, and only that.

'The first three verses of the poem show the confidence of the workmen in the power of art to overcome all evil spirits. They are possessed by the faith that the dead life is enriched in the measure in which they have enriched its tomb.

'In the last three verses of the poem the confidence of the workmen is shaken by the soul's experience, and the mummy herself now knows that the widow who cast her two mites into the treasury, which was all she had, had made the right preparation for death. Egyptian burial represents pre-Christian exaltation; resurrection in Wales represents Christian humility. Emerging from one into the other, the mummy has died, and is born.'

I should say something also about my ballads. The ballad form is, of course, as old as poetry itself, and one of the laws attaching to it seems to be that it must be hammered and beaten and knocked into shape until it is as hard and anonymous as a pebble on the shore.

My own ballads have a great deal in common with those of tradition. They are all rhythmical and intended to be read aloud; and in some I use a refrain. They are not in any sense private poems. Yet here the likeness ends. These ballads are elemental and they belong to myth, but they do not belong to history. In these it is not the narrative but the metaphysical situation that counts, and the symbols surrounding the situation.

VERNON WATKINS

You ask me to write a 'personal' note about my poems for the Society's *Bulletin* and I'll do my best in spite of the fact that I haven't got anything at all to say about these poems that the poems themselves don't – or ought not – to say. Of course it's the vast division between that 'don't' and 'ought not' that causes all my trouble. Since I really do not know what these poems are supposed to say, apart from the things that they do in fact say, it's a little difficult to speak. I've never been able to believe that poets invented or made up or created poems: it has always seemed to me that the poem allowed the poet to discover it much as a water diviner is permitted to come upon water. For this reason I don't see how the poet can have much to say about his own poems except in such terms as: 'This one is muddy but it's got a lot of iron in it' or 'I think I left part of this one still lying in the ground' or 'If you look closely at this poem you will see right the way down to Hell.'

I can, though, if you should wish it, give a few facts about the circumstances in which I discovered some of these poems. The first and longest, 'Goodman Jacksin and the Angel', derives its topography or setting from the situation of the old cottage in which I live here on the border of Sussex and Surrey. This cottage is set half a mile up an old public right of way through deep woods; and halfway along this lane, dividing Surrey from Sussex, stands the five-barred gate at which this dialogue of a farmer and an angel is supposed to happen. (There is a stud farm for racehorses on one side of this lane; I think that the figure of Goodman Jacksin is somewhat like the remarkable farmer who runs this stable. I think he is remarkable because I never met before a man who, if he set his mind to it, could breed a horse with wings or a unicorn.) This poem was written in six weeks of the winter of 1953 and was originally subtitled 'A theological Eclogue' but this was scrapped because it's really pretty obvious.

The one called 'The Mnemonic Demigod' is also about this old place I live in which is an Elizabethan woodcutter's cottage quite alone on the edge of a copse with a stream running round it and I don't think a brick or board of it has been touched by the hand of a builder (or decorator) since it was erected. And although no more than forty miles from London it's so remote that I often see wild foxes cross the meadow in front of me. The poem says: 'With Alworth over my head' and in fact this last home of Tennyson is the nearest house to my rickety retreat: he lived at the top of Blackdown and I live halfway up.

This note reads like an estate agent's catalogue but I have one more thing to say about Houses and this is to do with the poem about Longleat House. First of all this is erroneous – the name of the place is Longleat not Longleat House. The date has been added to the title because I visited the place not long after it left the possession of the Marquess of Bath and entered the possession of the National Trust.

There is a poem called 'Calendar Thoughts for the Month of the Dead' which was originally entitled 'Calendar Thoughts for February 1953'. I believe it was the Greeks who called February the Month of the Dead: I was born in it, and I know how right they were, so I changed it. Forgive the frivolity and futility of this note, which I cannot imagine being of service to anyone.

GEORGE BARKER

Autumn 1954   Collected Poems

I have written verses all my life, but very rarely a poem that goes on to the next page, and if it does it is generally one of my worst poems.

I am rather more satisfied with my late work than with my earlier, because on the whole it is simpler and more detached; though when I have been especially moved I think I have always written fairly simply. Nevertheless, to start writing in the Edwardian era was certainly a handicap for any minor poet, since at the back of our minds we carried a heavy cargo of affectations and half-dead poeticisms. On the other hand I am glad that a good deal of skill in manipulating words was expected from us as a matter of course, though any that I myself managed to acquire, alas did not come from a classical education, which my scientific family had not considered necessary. It came chiefly, I believe, from the endless poetry games I played as a child, above all with my brother Bernard Darwin, who was nine years older than me, and at that time an inspired writer of light verse. Our poetry game consisted in choosing six or eight words at random, and then having to fit these into a coherent verse or two, within ten minutes. I remember feeling quite sick sometimes with the effort to be worthy of my brother's ready and delightful praise, as well as my shame, when, although time was up, I had not been able to work in, say, the word *hippopotamus*.

My mother read me Elizabethan and seventeenth century lyrics when I was quite young, and I remember learning by heart, very early because I liked it so much, Sir Thomas Wyatt's:

> Forget not yet the tried intent
> Of such a truth as I have meant . . .

and delighting in Suckling's:

> If of herself she will not love,
> Nothing can make her:
> The devil take her!

This last seemed wonderfully daring to me. When I was about fourteen, my father introduced me to some of the poems of Swinburne and Browning. I was allergic to Swinburne, which rather puzzled me, because I had thought I should naturally always like the same things that he did. But Browning was a revelation to me. The line about the blue spurt of a lighted match made a small thunderclap in my mind. I suddenly saw that ordinary every-day experiences, such as I thought nobody but myself noticed, could become real poetry in a book. Later I used to sleep with a volume of Browning under my pillow, though the book sometimes seemed to have a great many corners in the middle of the night.

I gave no consideration to the verses I found myself writing from time to time, because the whole ambition of my youth was to be a painter, a career for which I was remarkedly ungifted.

The painter William Rothenstein was a friend of my parents, always very kind to me, interested and helpful, though at the same time he was never for one moment falsely encouraging. When I was a grown-up young woman I used sometimes to sit and draw with him in his studio, and he would talk to me about anything that came into his head. One day, agreeing with something or other he had said, I added: 'I've written a poem about that'. Afterwards he made me produce a few youthful lyrics from the bottom of my writing case, and then said: 'But this is what you ought to do'. Those eight words opened my eyes. Though I realised that he had overpraised what I had actually shown him, I saw from then on that verses came naturally to me and that painting did not.

Rothenstein persuaded my father to print privately my first volume of poems. Roger Fry reviewed it very kindly in *The Times Literary Supplement*, and it had a small *succès d'estime*.

By then I was married, and very glad to have found my own medium, since for a woman wanting to lead a usual domestic life, there is no form of creation so feasible as scribbling spontaneously on the backs of envelopes, and then struggling hard with the scribbles during quiet interludes of time.   FRANCES CORNFORD

I should like to thank the Poetry Book Society for the honour they have done me in choosing my book of poems, and to wish the reader enjoyment in reading them. Poems are written in enjoyment, or rather in a mixture of enjoyment and hard work. The reader should be exempted from the hard work. Some of these poems are 'personal', and came from some private feeling or actual happening. Others are shots at certain things which periodically trouble me, such as our origin and end, and the pattern of human life: perhaps I should call them return-shots, for the question must come from somewhere before one can make the response. From all I can learn, it is a common experience among poets to have some line occur to them spontaneously, almost capriciously, and this line, being a question, somehow or other then builds a poem round itself. About half the poems in this collection began in that way; the rest started from a general conception or subject which could be dealt with in a more systematic fashion. I imagine there is not much difference between the poems which began in these two separate ways, for the working on a poem seems to be what gives it character.

I have been asked to say something about poetry, and at the moment can think of nothing to say except that there can be no certain definition of poetry, and that if there were it would be of no conceivable use to anyone. One might as well demand a definition of mankind before setting out to become acquainted with people. We learn about poetry in much the same way as we learn about human beings, that is by coming to know it and them. There is this difference that in poetry enjoyment is the chief means of learning, as well as the reward for what we have learned. Judgement comes later, and it will probably come too soon: judgement is always something that has to be 'revised'; it is the uncertain factor in poetic matters, as in others, and it is the most important. If our judgement of poetry goes against our instinctive feelings, out of respect for an accepted judgement or for some theory, it will be false for us, though it may be true for others. We learn mostly from our own errors of feeling; but fortunately poetry has this compensation that it insensibly changes our feelings; in time they become wiser and begin to distinguish more justly between the false and the true, both in poetry and, I think, as a delayed result, in life as well.

EDWIN MUIR

Poetry and the Schools

I have never been very much in favour of introducing the work of living authors into school curricula of the study of English literature, for two reasons. First, I think that schoolboys and girls should be given a background of the classic authors of our language whose work is part of history and can be taught as such. Second, I think that all growing boys and girls should have an area of literature which they're not taught anything about, on which they don't have to pass any examinations, in which they can make their own discoveries, their own errors, and learn for themselves. If every secondary school in the country joined the Poetry Book Society and had a shelf in its library exhibiting the books of new poetry, this year and last year and several years, and just left them there for the boys and girls in the upper forms to discover for themselves and find out what they liked, we would be doing a very great service, because it is in the years between 14 and 18 if ever that people become readers of poetry and lovers of poetry, and also amongst those readers will be the poets of that generation. I think every poet has been a reader of poetry before he has been inflamed with the desire to become a writer of poetry, and it is a good thing also that boys and girls of that age should learn to think of poetry as a living art, as something which is still being written and which will be written in their own generation. I have always held firmly that a nation which ceases to produce poetry will in the long run cease to be able to enjoy and even understand the great poetry of its own past.

T. S. Eliot

Summer 1957   Poems of Many Years

Fifty years ago I did not forsee that I should become a poetical writer, but one day as I was by myself in our old village grammar-school the strange fascination of poetry seemed suddenly clear to me. Indeed, I had been brought up with plenty of books of poems at home, and knew many pieces by heart, but it was on one particular day that the chance opening of a small school anthology made me a complete devotee of poetry. In that collection Milton hurled Satan headlong from the ethereal sky and Thomson led the Father of the Tempest forth (much as I had observed in October over our hill) in black glooms.

When I tried to versify, it was to be expected that my subjects should often be from nature and the extensive village in which we lived. Of big towns and modern 'questions' I knew little. But it was hardly possible for any of us not to know something of our three rivers, each differing in character, of our hopfields and orchards and sheep-folds, and much else that was apparently eternal. If I wrote eagerly of these things it was not because I was following a group called 'The Georgians', though in the end Sir Edward Marsh found a place in his Georgian Anthology for poems of mine, but because my themes were daily experiences.

I would add however that from an early stage my notion of a poem was not that it should be just a transcript from nature, but was in part an experiment in style, a light from the writer's own resources of image and art upon the chosen moment and scene. The term 'nature poet' is honourable however limited in use, but it should not be taken to imply something like a verbal photographer.

Sometimes, in later years, I have fancied that I should compose one poetical study of nature and country affairs and characters all by itself; but other impulses have then distracted me from the plan, and verses on varied topics have intervened. These may now and then have met with kind and laudatory readers, but if someone says he or she still likes my 'pastorals' best, I am inclined to agree, and to look back fifty years to a childhood which explains this.

EDMUND BLUNDEN

Summer 1957   Roy Campbell *obit*. 22nd April 1957

'I feel our Bulletin would be incomplete without noticing the sudden and tragic death of Roy Campbell in a motoring accident in Portugal. This loss to English poetry cannot be replaced. The contemporary poetic stage is now robbed of its most adventurous and flamboyant figure. Ever since 1924, when he burst upon that stage, he maintained a singularly consistent role as inspired campaigner and champion of the under-dog, the ranker. Endowed with courage and great physical strength, he was able to perform feats which Byron would have envied, while his verse, like Byron's, carried the force and decisive edge of the man of action. The figure on the stage, who had cast himself so young for so romantic and heroic a part, was hardly more remarkable than the man in the wings himself talking with frankness and a disarming modesty in those intervals between episodes of aggressive action, and devoting himself with humility to his art and to his friends.

A firm friend, he was unswervingly loyal to his enemies, with whom he felt a communion like that a hunter feels with his prey. Dictatorship he despised as much as he loved tradition. Among his enemies those whom he alienated politically were the most deceived, for politics were not an integral part of Roy Campbell's consciousness. He looked for an heroic world, and in poetry for all that was heroic and divine in the imagination. When he did not find it he protested violently. He was bound to make sacrifices to his own myth.

Poetically Roy Campbell was the very opposite of Rilke; or it is perhaps truer to say that his type of courage was the very opposite of the type Rilke possessed. The one was active, positive, crusading; the other passive, receptive, enduring. Rilke did not recognize enemies, but to Roy Campbell, who saw everything as black or white, they were as dramatically necessary as the dragon was to Saint George. He was conscious, not only of an extreme poetic loneliness, but of an urgent sense of duty and of a need to daunt that Chimaera which represented to him the hesitant and the false.

Though born in South Africa, Roy Campbell was in the truest sense a European poet. His favourite country was Spain, which he knew better than any other. A friend of Lorca, he translated his plays and some of his poems; he told me that it was at the request of Lorca's parents that he decided to edit his works. His translations from Baudelaire and Rimbaud were, like those from Lorca, marked by his own accent, for his poetic idiom was too characteristic to be lost in translation. Whether he translated from French, Spanish or Portuguese, he brought his own masculine equipment to the service of works of whose subtlety he was acutely aware. When he sacrificed subtlety for force the choice was his own, and deliberately made. He had the keenest appreciation of what was magical and untranslatable in poetry, as he showed when he talked about Lorca's Canciones and the Poems of Gongora. He described the mastery and lyric perfection of Gongora as incomparable.

His translations from Saint John of the Cross, perhaps the finest he made, reveal an affinity of craftsmanship and of religious fervour which many who knew him only superficially might not have suspected. Accomplished though he was in the many fields of physical energy, he set the highest achievements of active life below the attainment of religious experience. Yet to the very end of his life both were linked in his imagination. His bullfighting, his horsemanship, and the part he took in the Spanish civil war, were inextricably linked in the pattern of his life. A postcard showing the Alcazar arrived from Toledo four days before his death, bearing these words: "I am having a wonderful time in this heavenly place which means more than all the world to me, because it was here that the Devil was routed in 1936 – as never before or since."'

VERNON WATKINS

Christmas 1957   Words for the Wind

It is an especial pleasure for an American to thank the Poetry Book Society for making *Words for the Wind* its Christmas choice.

The volume really consists of two books: earlier work and later. Since it is his last things which most interest a poet, let me dwell on these briefly.

I believe a book should reveal as many sides of a writer as is decent for him to show: that these aspects be brought together in some kind of coherent whole that is recognizable to the careful reader. This means that some poems will sometimes support other poems, either by being complements to them, or by providing contrasts. Thus, the first section of love poems in *Words for the Wind* contains pieces tender or highly romantic, others are 'witty', coarse and sensual. It is my hope that a reader will like both kinds of thing. Then by way of contrast, there is a handful of light pieces and poems for children. These are rougher than what most children's editors prefer. The attempt – part of a larger effort – was to make poems which would please both child and parent, without insulting the intelligence or taste of either.

The third section of these later pieces consists of poems of terror, and running away – and the dissociation of personality that occurs in such attempts to escape reality. In these the protagonist is alive in space, almost against his will; his world is the cold and dark known to sub-human things.

There follows a series of poems dedicated to W. B. Yeats. Highly formal stylistically, these poems are related to the sixteenth century, with lines severely end-stopped, for the most part.

Finally comes a sequence of longish poems 'Meditations of an Old Woman'. The protagonist is modelled, in part, after my own mother, now dead, whose favourite reading was the Bible, Jane Austen, and Dostoevsky – in other words a gentle, highly articulate old lady believing in the glories of the world, yet fully conscious of its evils.

These poems use a technique of developing themes alternately, a method employed in 'Praise to the End!', an earlier sequence, a kind of spiritual autobiography beginning with the very small child. Of these last poems I have said:

   ... Much of the action is implied or, particularly in the case of erotic experience, rendered obliquely. The revelation of the identity of the speaker may itself be a part of the drama; or, in some instance, in a dream sequence, his identity may merge with someone else's, or be deliberately blurred. This struggle for spiritual identity is, of course, one of the perpetual recurrences. (This is not the same as the fight of the adolescent personality for recognition in the 'real' world.) Disassociation often precedes a new state of clarity.

   Rhythmically, it's the spring and rush of the child I'm after – and Gammer Gurton's concision: *mutterchen's* wisdom. Most of the time the material seems to demand a varied short line. I believe that, in this kind of poem, the poet, in order to be true to what is most universal in himself, should not rely on allusion; should not comment or employ many judgment words; should not meditate (or maunder). He must scorn being 'mysterious' or loosely oracular, but be willing to face up to genuine mystery. His language must be compelling and immediate: he must create an actuality. He must be able to telescope image and symbol, if necessary, without relying on the obvious connectives: to speak in a kind of psychic shorthand when his protagonist is under great stress. He must be able to shift his rhythms rapidly, the 'tension'. He works intuitively, and the final form of his poem must be imaginatively right. If intensity has compressed the language so it seems, on early reading, obscure, this obscurity should break open suddenly for the serious reader who can hear the language: the 'meaning' itself should come as a dramatic revelation, an excitement. The clues will be scattered richly – as life scatters them; the symbols will mean what they usually mean – and sometimes something more ...

Words for the Wind opens with some very plain little bits of verse and descriptive pieces about a greenhouse I grew up in and around.

   But it is the longish pieces that really break the ground – if any ground is broken. And it is these that I hope the younger readers, in particular, will come to cherish. I think of myself as a poet of love, a poet of praise. And I wish to be read aloud.   THEODORE ROETHKE

21

Spring 1959   Edwin Muir *obit.* 3rd January 1959

Edwin Muir will be honoured as a man of fine, serious, unassuming character and a poet of most original and steadfast vision. We of the Poetry Book Society have additional cause to remember him, for he acted in 1954 as one of our first Selectors and two years later his book *One Foot in Eden* was acclaimed as our Spring Choice.

To say anything worth while the critic must leave safe generalities and ask what made Muir so singular a poet. He himself was constantly aware of the intimate relation between his waking and his dreaming world. But then, while every poet is grateful to receive gifts from the subconscious, Muir's role was more active. It is as if, plucking a golden bough, he descended into his underworld and faced its revelations not in a trance but with the concentrated gaze of a student, requiring them to yield sober truth. I feel that there is always the note of an inspired student, the rational Scottish mind working on an experience haloed with mystery which it could not deny.

A workaday world, shadowed and illumined by another: history fulfilled in fable: every individual an immortal spirit doomed to re-enact in variation the whole life of man, his own unconscious extending past the Fall to innocence, eternity, peace: intimations, beyond human time and space, of a close harmony between animal and man, a heraldic age in which 'the creatures went about' (I quote the *Autobiography*, essential to any full understanding of Muir's work) 'like characters in a parable of beasts.'

In such a linking of worlds Muir was absorbed. For him every event in time was burdened with meaning while, as to space, the bare Orkney island of his first seven years grew hiddenly to a universal landscape crossed by pilgrims of the past. The world of time and space was a betrayed world, a continual falling away, a corruption of the primal state. This complex vision excluded many delights; it had in it something oppressive, not allowing easy variety of tone and colour. But it was arresting in a unique manner, in the strange many-folded importance it gave to life. The style, lacking surface brilliance, matched the vision. It could be dry and fall into dullness of rhythm, but in its true quality it carried an intensity, a depth of suggestion, a subdued vividness and sometimes a sombre splendour.

For Muir himself the darkness of time and accelerating change was not unrelieved. The world of action was never far from the world of unmoving dream: into the latter he could step back, and there were charmed moments when the two were hardly to be separated. He was drawn, I think more and more, into Christianity. He still had one foot in Eden, but with his own gentle charity and humane reason he could not be blind to the presence of great good, as well as evil, in outcast Adam, for

> famished field and blackened tree
> Bear flowers in Eden never known.
> Blossoms of grief and charity
> Bloom in these darkened fields alone.
>
> GEORGE ROSTREVOR HAMILTON

Christmas 1960   Summoned by Bells

I have written verse for as long as I can remember. I have always preferred reading poetry to reading prose which is why I have found reviewing such an odious task – I read out loud to myself and cannot skip and this causes me to read slowly.

If we are influenced by the first poetry we read after the nursery rhymes we all know, I was influenced by W. E. Henley's *Lyra Heroica* which I was given at the age of about six or seven. I would not read blank verse in those days as I considered not using rhyme was cheating. I used to think then that you merely had to have the same number of syllables in each successive line to make correct scansion. I didn't find out about stress till I was about thirteen.

I have never thought one subject more 'poetical' than another, but have delighted in the niceties of rhyme and rhythm and choosing certain metres and rhyming schemes to suit certain subjects. A place or a moment recalls a mood I want to put down. A line comes to me. It gives me the beginnings of the rhythm for the poem. I put down the line on the nearest available bit of paper – the back of a cigarette packet or a letter (which consequently doesn't get answered) and think about the rest of the poem in trains, driving a motor car, bicycling or walking – wherever I can be alone and recite the words out loud until they seem to be the right ones in the right order. I write very slowly and copy the completed draft out five or six times before I am contented with it. Once this process is over, I am no longer interested in the verse.

I think everyone is a poet when young and that hearing and reading so much prose drives the poetry in most people underground. It then wells up again in the vast public memory for the words of popular songs. Much of my own verse has been written to the tunes of the

English Hymnal and Hymns A. & M. which are part of my heritage.

The fact that my verse has sold so well strikes me as lucky and miraculous for I think many living poets are better than I am. Please accept my thanks for choosing this blank verse autobiography.

JOHN BETJEMAN

Summer 1961   Weep Before God

Both as reader and writer, I have always enjoyed poetry and responded to it more deeply than to prose. There never was a time when my most fascinated and absorbed reading was not 'poetry' of one kind or another, starting from nursery rhymes and graduating to 'real' poetry by the recognised route – school, Shakespeare, Gray's Elegy, bits of French romantic verse suddenly perceived, amid the boredom of the classroom, to be *about* something. I was seventeen before it struck me that I myself might be a poet, but this I attribute to growing up in a *milieu* in which – for all its good points – one just didn't think of being a poet; that wasn't the kind of thing that happened.

It was Oxford that taught me that poetry was something that actually did get itself written, now, here, by people one might conceivably meet in the street. I began to write verse in 1943, but it was not until 1951 that any of my poems got into print (except, naturally, in the undergraduate papers in which everyone publishes). In that year, the University of Reading put out 120 copies of an elegant paperbound book, *Mixed Feelings*, containing nineteen poems. Nineteen poems ready for publication after eight years of writing verse? What kind of poet is this man? The answer is, a slow one. I noticed, early in life, that poets who write very copiously are usually either (a) no good at all or (b) very fine in a few of their poems and repetitive or uninspired in the rest. The best thing to aim at, in my opinion, was to write the few good poems and skip the many bad ones.

In this, I have naturally not succeeded. Although I have written a very small body of poetry (not more than fifty in my life that I 'wish to preserve'), quite a high proportion of it is bad. To write a good poem one needs a very special combination of energy, finesse, vividness of mood, directness of response to life, the right time, the right place, no distractions, and a lot of luck. If all those come together, and if one is a poet (which is not a profession but a condition), the bell rings. I have heard that bell ring precious few times in my life (those who dislike my

24

poetry would say, of course, that I have never heard it), and I would rather have that feeling than any other I have known.

For the rest, I believe that being a poet is a matter of avoiding two pitfalls. One is complacency, the kind that decides on an easy formula for being in the right (such as Identifying With the Working Class, or being religious, or not liking the hydrogen bomb, or knowing Latin and Greek) and then turns out verse to this formula, confident of its being good because it is founded on superior attitudes. Most of our self-conscious 'rebels' are bad poets of this kind. The other pitfall is intellectual laziness, which results in shoddy, imprecise writing. If one avoids these, and was born with the seeds of a poetic gift, there is always hope.

I haven't said anything about what my poems *say* – what kind of subject-matter I write about – because the poems themselves take care of that; and if they don't we might as well not take this any further.

JOHN WAIN

Autumn 1962   Collected Poems

Being asked to write about 'yourself and your poetry', I have to try to restrain myself from confidences that would be as embarrassing as superfluous. Like ordinary people, poets long to be loved. But all that is necessary is that they should be understood.

Whatever the value or success, or lack of them, of each individual poem, some intellectual effort has gone into all my verse, and I would beg a reader who has failed to get or be struck with (favourably or otherwise) anything I say to puzzle a little longer. I believe strongly in the virtue of poetry's allusive power. When Donne's readers saw 'snorted we in the seaven sleepers den' it was not only the alliteration and vowel sounds of the phrase that made it poetry but also the fact that they knew precisely who the 'sleepers' were. So a line of mine about living 'through wars of wanting neither side to win' is intended to pin down an aspect of this post-Second World War epoch, when the progressive forces have so often been tainted with dictatorship or terrorism. Again, I would like readers to wring the last ounce out of lines like:

> *Why the short sword of Brutus dealt*
> *A thrust at its beloved thing.*

The symbolism of 'short sword' (cf. 'short arm'); the physical envy and love-hatred of son for father in the Oedipus relation; the tradition that Brutus was Caesar's natural son – such things, as well as the situation of Shakespeare's play, are what I want the lines to convey.

Analysis can never harm a poem. My ideal reader would challenge every adjective, even in the most 'poetic' passage.

Far from the scarlet and sustaining lung.

'Scarlet' because one's experience in a butcher's shop or in drawing poultry has made one realise that 'lights' are the vividest red of any part of the body; and if the reader objects that the urban lung is soot-coloured, then I hope he will go on to realise that the lung of my poem belongs to a rural animal and is all the brighter for that. Above all, perhaps, the word suggests the lung as a generalized and idealized conception, the lung of the book on anatomy, for the pig of my poem is symbolical.

I have not meant to give the impression that my verse is difficult. It certainly does not set out to be. But in reading poetry, like listening to the monologue of a good comedian, nothing must be taken for granted:

The car in the lane that circumvents
The archipelagos of dung

(if I may choose a rather homely instance) – cow dung, obviously, because of its island shape; 'archipelagos' because of the tendency of a group of islands to consist of smaller and smaller islands at its extremity.

ROY FULLER

Christmas 1962   New Poems 1962

I have been publishing poems since the year 1909, since when I have watched a great many changes in fashion – names suddenly made and suddenly lost again, with here and there a real poet writing whom nobody pays much attention to, but who doesn't care because he's not competing with anyone but himself. It will always be that way.

The history of English poetry is traced in text-books as a succession of movements or schools – the School of Chaucer, the Allegorical School, the early Tudor Dramatists, the Euphuists and so on, past the Anti-Jacobins, the Lake School, the mid-Victorian romantics, until one reaches the Georgians, the Imagists and the Modernist Movement, for which the bell is now tolling. But schools and movements are fictions. If a school, meaning the disciples and imitators of a particular verse-craftsman or technician, achieves newspaper renown, this is a grave criticism of his sincerity. A poet should be inimitable. When two real poets recognize each other as true to their common vocation, this will only accentuate the difference between them in rhythm, diction and the rest. Any talk of a 'school' means that someone is peddling a new technique of verbal conjuring; as in commercial schools that teach writers of advertising copy how to make easily hypnotizable subjects believe what they themselves never believe in. Craftsmanship is self taught by the poet's service to the Muse: who is unpossessable and never satisfied.

A poet needs constant discouragement. I like to think that this Poetry Book Society choice of my new poems is a simple act of alms-giving: and indeed, not having been gainfully employed or licked an insurance stamp in all my life, I am unentitled to the Old Age Pension.

ROBERT GRAVES

Autumn 1963   The Burning Perch

When I assembled the poems in *The Burning Perch* (I am not happy about the title but could not think of anything better), I was taken aback by the high proportion of sombre pieces, ranging from bleak observations to thumbnail nightmares. The proportion is far higher than in my last book, *Solstices*, but I am not sure why this should be so. Fear and resentment seem here to be serving me in the same way as Yeats in his old age claimed to be served by 'lust and rage', and yet I had been equally fearful and resentful of the world we live in when I was writing *Solstices*. All I can say is that I did not set out to write this kind of poem: they happened. I am reminded of Mr Eliot's remark that the poet is concerned not only with beauty but with 'the boredom and the horror and the glory'. In some of the poems in *The Burning Perch* the boredom and the horror were impinging very strongly, e.g. the former in *Another Cold May* or *October in Bloomsbury* and the latter in *Flower Show*, *After the Crash*, *Charon* or *Budgie*. I find, however, that in most of these poems the grim elements are mixed with others, just as they are hardly any examples of pure satire in this collection; *This is the Life*, I suppose, comes nearest to it but still seems to me no more purely satirical than, for example, a medieval gargoyle.

27

When I say that these poems 'happened', I mean among other things that they found their own form. By this I do not, of course, mean that the form was uncontrolled: some poems chose fairly rigid patterns and some poems loose ones but, once a poem had chosen its form, I naturally worked to mould it to it. Thus, while I shall always be fond of rhyme and am sorry for those simpleminded people who proclaim that it is now outmoded (after all it remains unbeatable for purposes of epigram), a good third of the poems in this book are completely without it. Similarly with rhythm: I notice that many of the poems here have been trying to get out of the 'iambic' groove which we were all born into. In *Memoranda to Horace* there is a conscious attempt to suggest Horatian rhythms (in English of course one cannot do more than suggest them) combined with the merest reminiscence of Horatian syntax. This technical Horatianizing appears in some other poems too where, I suppose, it goes with something of a Horatian resignation. But my resignation, as I was not brought up a pagan, is more of a fraud than Horace's: *Memoranda to Horace* itself, I hope, shows this. So here again, as in poems I was writing thirty years ago (I myself can see both the continuity and the difference), there are dialectic, oxymoron, irony. I would venture the generalisation that most of these poems are two-way affairs or at least spiral ones: even in the most evil picture the good things, like the sea in one of these poems, are still there round the corner.

LOUIS MACNEICE

[EDITOR'S NOTE: *This contribution by Louis MacNeice must have been one of the last things he wrote before his death on 3 September 1963. He sent it with a letter dated August 26th, apologising for delay and saying 'my doctor won't let me go to London yet, so everything is awkward.'*]

Spring 1964   The Whitsun Weddings

It would, perhaps, be fitting for me to return the heartening compliment paid by the Selectors to *The Whitsun Weddings* with a detailed annotation of its contents. Unfortunately, however, once I have said that the poems were written in or near Hull, Yorkshire, with a succession of Royal Sovereign 2B pencils during the years 1955 to 1963, there seems little to add. I think in every instance the effect I was trying to get is clear enough. If sometimes I have failed, no marginal annotation will help now. Henceforth the poems belong to their readers, who will in due course pass judgment by either forgetting or remembering them.

If something must be said, it should be about the poems one writes not necessarily being the poems one wants to write. Some years ago I came to the conclusion that to write a poem was to construct a verbal device that would preserve an experience indefinitely by reproducing it in whoever read the poem. As a working definition, this satisfied me sufficiently to enable individual poems to be written. Insofar as it suggested that all one had to do was pick an experience and preserve it, however, it was much over-simplified. Nowadays nobody believes in 'poetic' subjects, any more than they believe in poetic diction. The longer one goes on, though, the more one feels that some subjects *are* more poetic than others, if only that poems about them get written whereas poems about other subjects don't. At first one tries to write poems about everything. Later on, one learns to distinguish somewhat, though one can still make enormously timewasting mistakes. The fact is that my working definition defines very little: it makes no reference to this necessary element of distinction, and it leaves the precise nature of the verbal pickling unexplained.

This means that most of the time one is engaged in doing, or trying to do, something of which the value is doubtful and the mode of operation unclear. Can one feel entirely happy about this? The days when one could claim to be the priest of a mystery are gone: today mystery means either ignorance or hokum, neither fashionable qualities. Yet writing a poem is still not an act of the will. The distinction between subjects is not an act of the will. Whatever makes a poem successful is not an act of the will. In consequence, the poems that actually get written may seem trivial or unedifying, compared with those that don't. But the poems that get written, even if they do not please the will, evidently please that mysterious something that has to be pleased.

This is not to say that one is forever writing poems of which the will disapproves. What it does mean, however, is that there must be among the ingredients that go towards the writing of a poem a streak of curious self-gratification, almost impossible to describe except in some such terms, the presence of which tends to nullify any satisfaction the will might be feeling at a finished job. Without this element of self-interest, the theme, however worthy, can drift away and be forgotten. The situation is full of ambiguities. To write a poem is a pleasure: sometimes I deliberately let it compete in the open market, so to speak, with other spare-time activities, ostensibly on the grounds that if a poem isn't more entertaining to write than listening to records or going out it won't be entertaining to read. Yet doesn't this perhaps conceal a subconcious objection to writing? After all, how many of our pleasures really bear thinking about? Or is it just concealed laziness?

Whether one worries about this depends, really, on whether one is more interested in writing or in finding how poems are written. If the former, then such considerations become just another technical difficulty, like noisy neighbours or one's own character, parallel to a clergyman's doubts: one has to go on in spite of them. I suppose in raising them one is seeking some justification in the finished product for the sacrifices made on its behalf. Since it is the will that is the seeker, satisfaction is unlikely to be forthcoming. The only consolation in the whole business, as in just about every other, is that in all probability there was really no choice.

PHILIP LARKIN

Summer 1964   Joseph Compton *obit.* 27th Feb. 1964

Jo Compton was an ideal chairman of this Society. In the art itself he had absolutely no axes to grind, and though his sympathies were wide he had a sure nose for the phoney, the impossibly amateur, and the pretentious. On the other hand he was extraordinarily receptive to new work: he kept up with his reading and had a very shrewd idea of what was going on even in the tiniest of little magazines. In committee he was first class: business was got through expeditiously but there was always time for jokes and scandal (often of his own purveying) and decisions taken were decisions of the whole committee (though he might well have unobtrusively put it right on matters of possibility and fairness). Outside committee, in negotiating for money and support, and taking spot decisions on day to day problems, he was skilful and wise. It is notoriously difficult to 'help' poetry: JC found several new ways and himself encouraged their development and change. The English Festival of Spoken Poetry was a typical example. This was started primarily to set standards in verse speaking for teachers and drama students. But JC brought young poets in among the judges and saw to it that good modern poems were among the set pieces. So that in these and other ways what might have merely been a worthy but pedagogic occasion had a real creative streak running through it. And he himself provided the vision and drive (and secured the finance) to transform the Festival into the general festivals at the Mermaid and the Royal Court, run by the Poetry Book Society (itself transformed for that purpose!). His enthusiasm for the Society never cooled. He was especially keen that schools should become members. This was not just because of his career as an educationalist: he simply believed that reading poetry ought to be part of everyone's life. He was in severe pain when he conducted his last meetings of the Society's Board: it was distressing to see the changes made by his illness in one who had been a connoisseur of travel and food and wine as well as the arts. But the meetings went on with the old efficiency and good humour, and the constant concern from the chair for the dissemination of poetry and the material well-being of its practitioners.

ROY FULLER

Christmas 1964   This Cold Universe

If you intend to compose or paint there are various great academies to teach students techniques and offer styles and disciplines. No 'singing schools' exist for poetry. A poet must read omnivorously and continuously all the great masters of his sedentary trade, and a far wider range of contemporaries than he thinks he can bear. He must keep in training if ever he is to dare be confident enough to say, like Yeats, 'words obey my call'. Poets are not compelled to publish. If asked why they do (publishers willing) I think mostly they'd say they wanted to communicate because they had things they thought worthwhile, which couldn't be communicated in any other way than in a poem. I can think of no better notion than Robert Frost's that a poem is a small 'clarification of life' or at least a 'stay against confusion'. I've hoped, too, that my poems will give pleasure. This word covers the fullest recognition by unknown readers of whatever situations the poems offer. '*Sunt lacrumae rerum, et mentem mortalia tangunt.*' There is a magical pleasure in this line of Vergil's both because its expression is perfect – the meaning wholly in twin with rhythm and sound, and vice versa – and because, though the meaning is wholly clear, it lives in the rhythm and sound and cannot be divorced into a cold prose nisi. The definition of what poetry is exists in the rhythms of such poetry in any language. Unlike most poets I have earned most of my adult life by presenting in public in various ways the work of other poets of all ages and styles 'past and passing and to come'. I am confident that in this I *have* given

31

much proper pleasure. I've been asked if this harms my poetry. On the contrary the deeper the explorations into others' work the more fruitful. I have learned a great deal about the nature of poetry: what a poem 'is' and 'means'. And why Wordsworth wrote 'we murder to dissect'. Poems are what they say; which is not always what the poet intended. I have explored to the essence of many poems in a way a reader *need* not, have got near to what the poet aimed to communicate. I have always felt, in so working on a poem in order to offer it to others, that I was the first reader of it – always therefore exhilarated and excited, and chastened into some disciplined delight: contriving to have the poem say all it said and imply all the poet meant to say, perhaps failed to. These self imposed identifications with poets, often antipathetic, but of inviolable worth, have given me an objective insight and a strict catholicity which I know has brought my own work to whatever value it has to others. I have learnt through a long, loving, and practical dealing with poetry not to be doctrinaire or dogmatic. The increasing knowledge of what I write in relation to poetry in general does not dismay; my predilection for all sorts of other people's poetry does not prevent but rather prompts me to my own; my continually living contacts with all English poetry (and my missionary zeal) has allotted me a rather isolated position foes might call arrogance; friends independence. I've never cared for schools or movements because I've found by experience that, over two thousand years, poets are individuals. But it is not wholly from practical experience that I am utterly opposed to Robert Graves's idea that a poet's work should not be allied to his art. In my time I have been a selector for the Poetry Book Society; I've known the cramps of the job. For me it is an especial source of gratification to be a Choice, particularly as I think my own ways of living with and in others' work has in fact refined and sharpened and directed my own way of writing poetry. I have one wish – I think many members of the Poetry Book Society would share – I wish I could have shared my pleasure in this Choice with Joe Compton. One can't 'do' much for poetry. He did all he could. Poetry is not the addition and subtraction of its critics. It is the multiplication and division of those who like it. He was a multiplier.

PATRIC DICKINSON

Spring 1965   Ariel by Sylvia Plath

In her earlier poems, Sylvia Plath composed very slowly, consulting her Thesaurus and Dictionary for almost every word, putting a slow, strong ring of ink around each word that attracted her. Her obsession with intricate rhyming and metrical schemes was part of the same process. Some of those early inventions of hers were almost perverse, with their bristling hurdles. But this is what she enjoyed. One of her most instinctive compulsions was to make patterns – vivid, bold, symmetrical patterns. She was fond of drawing – anything, a blade of grass, a tree, a stone, but preferably something complicated and chaotic, like a high heap of junk. On her paper this became inexorably ordered and powerful, like a marvellous piece of sculpture, and took on the look of her poems, everything clinging together like a family of living cells, where nothing can be alien or dead or arbitrary. The poems in *Ariel* are the fruits of that labour. In them, she controls one of the widest and most subtly discriminating vocabularies in the modern poetry of our language, and these are poems written for the most part at great speed, as she might take dictation, where she ignores metre and rhyme for rhythm and momentum, the flight of her ideas and music. The words in these odd-looking verses are not only charged with terrific heat, pressure and clairvoyant precision, they are all deeply related within any poem, acknowledging each other and calling to each other in deep harmonic designs. It is this musical, almost mathematical hidden law, which gives these explosions their immovable finality.

Behind these poems there is a fierce and uncomprising nature. There is also a child desperately infatuated with the world. And there is a strange muse, bald, white and wild, in her 'hood of bone', floating over a landscape like that of the Primitive Painters, a burningly luminous vision of a Paradise. A Paradise which is at the same time eerily frightening, an unalterably spot-lit vision of death.

And behind them, too, is a long ardous preparation. She grew up in an atmosphere of tense intellectual competition and Germanic rigour. Her mother, first-generation American of Austrian stock, and her father, who was German-Polish, were both University teachers. Her father, whom she worshipped, died when she was nine, and thereafter her mother raised Sylvia and her brother single-handed. Whatever teaching methods were used, Sylvia was the perfect pupil:

33

she did every lesson double. Her whole tremendous will was bent on excelling. Finally, she emerged like the survivor of an evolutionary ordeal: at no point could she let herself be negligent or inadequate. What she was most afraid of was that she might come to live outside her genius for love, which she also equated with courage, or 'guts', to use her word. This genius for love she certainly had, and not in the abstract. She didn't quite know how to manage it: it possessed her. It fastened her to cups, plants, creatures, vistas, people, in a steady ecstasy. As much of all that as she could, she hoarded into her poems, into those incredibly beautiful lines and hallucinatory evocations.

But the truly miraculous thing about her will remain the fact that in two years, while she was almost fully occupied with children and house-keeping, she underwent a poetic development that has hardly any equal on record, for suddeness and completeness. The birth of her first child seemed to start the process. All at once she could compose at top speed, and with her full weight. Her second child brought things a giant step forward. All the various voices of her gift came together, and for about six months, up to a day or two before her death, she wrote with the full power and music of her extraordinary nature.

Ariel is not easy poetry to criticise. It is not much like any other poetry. It is her. Everything she did was just like this, and this is just like her – but permanent.

TED HUGHES

Spring 1965   T. S. Eliot *obit.* 4th January 1965

It is impossible in a few paragraphs to discuss Eliot's work. But it may be of interest to members of the Poetry Book Society if I try to say something about his attitude towards writing poetry.

Realism is a word used to connote work that is representational. But every vital movement in art is in fact a new approach to reality. When Eliot started publishing poetry before the first world war, most of the poets then writing – the Georgians – had an idea of poetry and the poet as being apart from life – especially from modern life. The world around them had to conform to their idea of poetry which was derived, essentially, from the Romantics. Experience which was not poetic did not fit their conventions of vocabulary, form and subject matter. So it was ignored or condemned. The best of their writing –

and in de la Mare and Housman it was very good indeed – turned towards dreams or death or the countryside as an escape from the town and materialism.

Eliot thought of poetry as a medium for discussing seriously what modern men and women are serious about: even though (and this is where complexity comes in) what they take as seriously is often trivial, and has to be treated ironically – certainly without solemnity. The link between the poet and an audience which does not seem to care about poetry, is that the poetry of people's lives is lived out in extremely unpoetic symbols; the car, the gasworks, the cinema – whatever is the subject of their dreams. Beauty, terror and loneliness act out their dramas in images drawn from modern life. The poet, unless he is to cut himself off from the roots of living in our world, cannot turn away from these things and confine himself to the subjects, vocabulary and forms which are those of his predecessors, and which appear to be the currency of the poetic.

At the same time, the idea that poetry has to involve itself in a language of discourse about the modern world which people in that world take seriously, is the most superficial aspect of Eliot's work. It shows in poems like *Preludes* and *Morning at the Window* which do little more than prove that poetry can be made of the apparent ugliness of modern life. He did not reject the past. On the contrary, he thought of past poetry as expressing the supreme moments of consciousness in language – language being that activity of human beings in which time and death counts least. In their writings the dead speak directly to us, are part of our own lives. For poets the problem of being contemporary is how, in our different circumstances, we can converse with them in that debate between the living and the dead which is literature.

Eliot (as, of course, also Joyce and Pound) substituted for the idea of tradition as simply the extension of certain conventions of the poetic from fathers to sons – from Swinburne, let us say, to J. C. Squire – the idea of the accessibility of the whole past of English literature to us if it served our own poetic purposes. Instead of thinking of Tennyson and Swinburne and the Georgians as traditional writers because they were the nearest successors to us from a further past, the whole past was regarded as available. Language was at it were taken out of history and regarded as contemporaneous to every poet alive who took the trouble to master English. All the poets, from Chaucer to Tennyson were voices in the next room. And some of them – the

35

Elizabethans and Dryden and Donne – were seen to be closer to our problems which require clear imagery and hard thinking, than the Victorians.

His craftsmanship was prodigious, but its importance to him can be exaggerated if one thinks of his poetry as an entirely conscious process. He retained a sense of the mystery of poetry. He analysed in his criticism, and in his poetry he was to some extent a critic. Nevertheless ultimately he abided by the mystery, by the idea of poetry as language 'rich and strange', of analysis as being a set of devices in order to realise in the poetry rhythm, music and imagery that are unanalysable. When everything that can be has been explained about Eliot we are confronted with the inexplicable, or – to put it more fashionably – with the unconscious elements. The key to his greatness lies in his combination of great intellectual power with a deep respect for the mysteries.

STEPHEN SPENDER

[EDITORIAL NOTE: *Mr T. S. Eliot was a founder member of the Poetry Book Society and served as a director during 1954 and 1955.*]

Christmas 1965   The Hollow Hill

My view of poetry is that of tradition, and in absolute opposition to any poetic theories whose foundation is the positivist humanism so widespread at the present time. I would go so far as to say that the arts (normally the language of man's metaphysical and spiritual knowledge) are finally incompatible with these philosophies. I assent to Dante's definition of poetry as the writing of 'beautiful things truly', to Coomaraswamy's 'art is expression informed by ideal beauty'; to Blake's 'One thing alone makes a poet – Imagination, the Divine Vision'; to Yeats's 'Supreme art is a traditional statement of certain heroic and religious truths, passed on from age to age, modified by individual genius but never **abandoned**'; or indeed to Dom Bede Griffiths's belief that the function of the arts is 'to evoke the divine presence'; to A.E. when he says 'It is certain that metrics as a mode of speech correspond to something in the soul. But if we say this we are impelled to deny the fitness of verse utterance of any feeling, imagination or reverie which has not originated in the magic fountain'; to Plotinus's 'the soul itself acts immediately, affirming the Beautiful

36

where it finds something accordant with the ideal form within itself. But let the soul fall in with the ugly and at once it shrinks within itself, denies the thing, turns away from it, not accordant, resenting it'; and in consequence, to the conclusion that 'one of the very first symptoms of the loss of the soul is the loss of the sense of beauty'.

I am in fact (in the tradition of Spenser, Vaughan and Traherne, Coleridge, Shelly, Yeats and all imaginative poets) a Platonist; and (in consequence, since that philosophy implies the concordance of visible with invisible forms) a symbolist. Among modern English poets I admire chiefly Yeats, Edwin Muir, Vernon Watkins and David Gascoyne. That the poems I have written will survive the test of these values I hesitate to hope; but if not, it is the poems and not the ground of poetry which are to be discarded.

KATHLEEN RAINE

Christmas 1966   The Force and Other Poems

When I was given the Gregory Fellowship at Leeds University, people, some people, said to me 'All your life you've begged, borrowed and embezzled time from your employers to do your own work. Surely this robber's life was itself a stimulus, and now you won't know how to fill the time', for the Fellowship gives an annual stipend and asks no formal duties in return – only that the painter, sculptor or poet should, so far as he is able, pursue his own work.

I had no doubt in my mind that writing was not an occasional thing for me, but the thing with which I felt out the world, a sense organ combined of, and worth more than, all the others put together. So I did work, and was still working when my two years came to an end, hard enough to ask for another year, which the University was generous enough to give me. And I was doubly pleased, first when my publishers gave me the opportunity to collect the three years' work into a volume, and secondly to have some warranty that it was working as a body when it was picked by the Poetry Book Society.

I have no illusions that in the perspective of time the real poems are few and far between, and those who anybody thinks have written them change places very rapidly. There is no accolade in anybody's lifetime. But the poet like any other artist wants to keep on working, discovering and fashioning these intense wholenesses which he believes in. And the poet is something of an outsider even in artistic society. He is scarcely thought of as a working artist, somebody who has to spend daily hours in his studio if he is to accomplish anything. It is rare for him to be able to show himself as a working man on the same footing as painters or sculptors, he making verbal objects. And here I must pay tribute to the other Gregory Fellows at that time, Dennis Creffield and Neville Boden, painter and sculptor respectively, who had the clarity of mind to treat a poet like any other artist, and the generosity and friendliness to admit him into their Fellowship.

As for the poems in *The Force*, I have implied above that I believe them to be a step forward in my work towards conscious art, partly because (as one hopes) one grows, and partly because of the working conditions I was lucky enough to be in when I was writing the poems. There is I think a stronger tendency to show thought in action, and to draw upon conjecture, than in my other books. This does not necessarily make them better *poems*, but assuming they *are* any good, it is likely to make them larger poems. I have a feeling that literature in the progress of any civilisation begins with myth (I do not mean by myth an interesting falsehood, but a discovered mental fact, and I include the religious myths) and ends with myth. This explains the otherwise perhaps puzzling attribution to certain science fiction journals in the front pages of *The Force*, since SF is one of the great repositories of myth in our time, and it is precisely so important because it incorporates the scientific facts of twentieth century existing into its mythology. The initials can equally well stand for *Science Folklore*. I am moved that the journals concerned have thought that certain of my work draws upon these important forces, images of time and relative time, of absolute size and relative significance, of the impingement of still unspecified and apparently personal forces on a world that was once thought by science to be entirely material.

And as for choosing that title *The Force* for the book, this is the force that spins the world (or does not, as we choose), called love.

PETER REDGROVE

A, a, a Domine Deus

I said, Ah! what shall I write?
I enquired up and down.
   (He's tricked me before
with his manifold lurking-places.)
I looked for His symbol at the door.
I have looked for a long while
   at the textures and contours.
I have run a hand over the trivial intersections.
I have journeyed among the dead forms
causation projects from pillar to pylon.
I have tried the eyes of the mind
   regarding the colours and lights.
I have felt for His Wounds
   in nozzles and containers.
I have wondered for the automatic devices.
I have tested the inane patterns
   without prejudice.
I have been on my guard
   not to condemn the unfamiliar.
For it is easy to miss Him
   at the turn of a civilisation.
 I have watched the wheels go round in case
I might see the living creatures like the appearance of lamps, in case I might see the Living
God projected from the Machine. I have said to
the perfected steel, be my sister and for the
glassy towers I thought I felt some beginnings
of His creature, but *A, a, a, Domine Deus*, my
hands found the glazed work unrefined and
the terrible crystal a stage-paste . . . *Eia,
Domine Deus.*

DAVID JONES

To put together one's *Collected Poems* is a strange experience; it entails both a backward glance at all one has already written and also a forward look at what may be one's future verse. In both cases, it is the revelation of the mind and heart of a particular person.

On putting my *Collected Poems* together, I was vividly aware of two things: The effect of the influence of other poets on my work (Graves, Auden, Eliot, Yeats, Muir and Wallace Stevens), and the formation of a personal style and subject matter. For me, poetry has always been a way of discovery of the truth, both in myself and in the world around me. In the most literal sense, I do not know what I think until I see what I write.

I started writing verse at the age of thirteen and for me, then, the music and movement of my poems were the most important factors. I was too inexperienced to have very much to write about; what concerned me above all else was the ability to make a poem rhyme and scan. 'The rest', as Eliot said in a very different context, 'was not my business'.

As I grew up, I came strongly under the influence of Auden and Eliot; I began to write more freely, imagining that by writing a looser kind of verse I was using Eliot's great and subtle *vers libre*. But I needed this poet's sense of discipline and this I lacked for several years. Yet I *was* learning other forms of discipline from Edwin Muir and W. H. Auden. From Muir, I aquired a knowledge of how to handle allegory in modern verse. Muir showed me how to *find* my own world, I was not merely inhabiting it. Auden and Yeats did something of the same thing. For me, poetry, ever since this time, has been among many other things, the creation of a world and also a way of knowledge.

In my teens, I came to use verse in a confessional manner; it was an outlet for my secret thoughts and longed-for ecstasies. It was not, therefore, of much value in its own right. There was one useful quality it did have, however, and that was that it gave me experience as an apprentice-poet, as one who was attempting to learn how to handle form, music, metaphor and simile. For this reason, I am not sorry that I wrote, while still very young, a great many ephemeral poems. These poems enabled me to write, when I became more experienced, simply and directly of experiences from far deeper levels. In my *Collected Poems* I have tried to include the best both of my earlier and later work.

My *Collected Poems* pose the whole question of originality in verse-writing. How much does one owe to others and how much is entirely one's own? Virginia Woolf wrote in *Letter to a Young Poet* of the debt which all writers owed to those of the past. T. S. Eliot wrote of much the same thing and reiterated it more than once. Myself, I am no longer acutely aware of past influences. What does concern me, however, is the consciousness at times of repeating myself, of using the same tone of voice too often, or of repeating the same things.

To produce a volume of *Collected Poems* may seem rather final, a sort of summing-up. This has never seemed to me to be the case with this book of mine. Some of the poems, it is true, do seem quite strange to me; others appear very familiar. *All* of them are an important part of my life and of my future. A little of every poem in this book contains part of my own essential self. For this reason, each one is especially precious to me. I can only hope that they will appear so to other people. A *Collected Poems* after all demands an audience in an especially serious way.

ELIZABETH JENNINGS

Christmas 1967   Vernon Watkins *obit.* 10th Oct. '67

But for his waves of gentle white hair and something otherwordly about a 20's Cambridge intonation, Vernon Watkins was a young man in thought and deed. His son, he told me, had always been years older than him. Just as he never compromised his poetry to the London scene or a career in copywriting or the campus, so he was destined not to know the compromises of middle-age in his life. He died young and in full flight, albeit at sixty-one. His death is sad for more than the usual reasons.

We met at Newton Abbot Station in Somerset last November, not for the Races but a poetry reading tour of six towns in the South-West. I was the full supporting cast. When I first saw him he was walking smartly away from me down a platform where he had been waiting several hours in the rain, having caught an earlier train 'in case of floods'. His resemblance to Don Quixote is almost too obvious to mention. He was buckled tightly into a Burberry with a protective trilby slanted over his beaked fastidious face. From under his hat at the back had fallen a piece of hair like a long feather. In his hand was a paper bag of shrimps which he had caught that morning below his beloved cliff house near Swansea. He immediately offered me one. At

41

the social tea we were then invited to he shared them round between the cakes. He had a kind of zany chivalry which made people love him rather to his politely withheld surprise.

He had certainly never heard of me but insisted on equal reading time always, so while he read different poems each night from an entire life's work, he was obliged to hear my entire output repeated monotonously wherever we went. To prove he wasn't bored he even asked to read them for himself. Grace, in all senses, was one of his first qualities. He lived, ate, drank and spoke poetry and only for poetry. It's an uncommon and exhilarating preoccupation.

I was travelling with wife and baby in a hire car and each morning I'd collect him from his night's host and we'd meander off through Autumn Devonshire in the vague direction of our next stand, like a couple of boy scouts on a scavenge hunt. It was the greatest fun and it is with a sadness new to me that I remember his unguarded friendliness, his darting, open mind, the way he would screw his head round suddenly to see a signpost or a bird, and the unassuming way in which he assumed himself to be of interest – in long, hilarious, passenger-seat monologues – solely for his friendship with the ever-present 'Dylan'. He was wrong in that respect. Like Don Quixote, he was a cockeyed optimist, lovable and rare. I was honoured to be his part-time Sancho Panza on that, his one but last mission.

HUGO WILLIAMS

Spring 1968   Underneath the Water

For me, the central problem in writing is the age-old one of communication. There's not much point in talking on a dead line. 'Simplify, simplify,' wrote Thoreau. But at just what point does one stop, and allow suggestibility to take over? Every poem is a venture along a knife-edge towards that exact degree of simplification.

The effect of a poem (but not necessarily its 'meaning', whatever that implies) should be instantaneous. At the same time, the poem should conceal certain properties that may only reveal themselves very gradually. It's not the business of the poet to allow a poem, at a first reading, to burn itself out in one brilliant flash. The poem must have something in reserve; it must be capable of showing fresh aspects of its nature to reader as well as to writer, perhaps over a period of years of reading and re-reading.

Poetry, to me, has always been a special kind of autobiography. In the process of writing it, something highly personal has – somehow – to be universalised. I'd hope that the poems in *Underneath the Water* together form a unity, and aren't merely a lot of fragments. This hope may very well be forlorn, for the poet is the last man on earth to judge the total effect of a new collection of his own work: he is too near, and already too far, from what he has written.

Apart from the years 1940-1947, I have lived all my life in Launceston, a small Cornish market-town. Since 1947,* I have worked as a teacher (all subjects from religious education to disorganised games) mainly with children under the age of twelve. As a child, I went to the same school where I now work: a rather grim-looking building put up in 1840 on the rim of the borough allotments.

It's not surprising, then, that several poems in *Underneath the Water* are concerned with childhood: my own, and of those I try to 'teach' – always conscious of Bernard Shaw's maxim that he who attempts to 'mould' a child's character is the worst type of abortionist. I am also concerned to examine, and re-examine, the mythology of my own town, whose stones I sometimes think I know too well for comfort. Two other obsessive themes I hope I shall now never escape are those of the war and the sea. It was Brendan Behan who described his neuroses as the 'nails and saucepans' of his trade, and expressed not the slightest wish to be free of them. I share the sentiment.

I think I became a working poet the day I joined the destroyer *Eclipse* at Scapa Flow in August, 1940. Though I wrote only fragmentary notes for the next three years, the wartime experience was a catalytic one. I knew that at last I had found my first subject, as well as a form. Living and working on the lower-deck meant that if I was to write anything at all, then it would have to be in the kind of shorthand of experience (to use a horrible phrase) poetry happens to be.

I've tried to go on doing this. I write my poems slowly, at about the speed of coral; and I recognise that this slowness of pace may be equally as dangerous as writing quickly. But I feel that one of the poet's greatest dangers is the impatience that Goëthe warns against: 'We must be right by nature so that good thoughts may come before us like free children of God, and cry "Here we are!"''

I am profoundly grateful to the Poetry Book Society selectors for having chosen *Underneath the Water*. All too often the poet has the feeling he is merely talking to himself. It is a relief, and one of the best sorts of encouragement, sometimes to know otherwise.

CHARLES CAUSLEY

* In 1976 Charles Causley resigned from his teaching post

When the centenary of the birth of W. B. Yeats was celebrated in 1965, there were many pleasant literary gatherings in Dublin and elsewhere. The main event was the re-opening of the Tower at Ballylee, which had been restored carefully and with taste. This was due to the efforts of the local Kiltartan Society, which obtained a Government grant. I had been at Ballylee some years previously and it was a desolate spot: cattle sheltered in the lower chamber of the Tower: the wall plaster, which had been painted a deep cobalt, was peeling off; south west winds had blown down many of the sea-green slates from the roof. Even the double cottage in which the poet stayed – for the Tower itself was too damp – was in ruins. I followed a stream which flowed into the little river nearby and found that it came from under the road and made my way past thorn-trees and saw, a hundred yards away, that the stream was linked with the river again. Yeats, who was shorted-sighted, did not venture into marsh or brake and had not realised that his Tower was on an island. Otherwise he might have written about his moat for he was always fascinated by islands ever since he wrote in early youth, *The Island of Statues*.

Our doyen poet, Padraic Colum, friend of Synge and Joyce, came from New York to deliver the opening address. On the next morning I read out some of the poems of Yeats in the Tower and in the afternoon I spoke some more under the bust of Maeceanas in the great Pleasure Garden at Coole. Here there was still desolation: rose bushes gone wild, flowers hidden among deepening weeds. When the small crowd had left, I lingered on for I wanted to test an unfinished poem which Yeats had written about an echo from a corner of the high wall on the opposite side of the garden. I called out and, sure enough, the lonely inhabitant of that waste answered me. Hence the title of this book.

During that centenary year, poetry seemed to be of some public importance again and that feeling inspired writers here. I wrote several poems as a tribute to Yeats and followed them with other poetic memories of AE, Joyce, James Stephens, and F. R. Higgins, from whose knowledge of western folk lore and ballads Yeats borrowed in his last poems. These poems are included in this book.

Austin Clarke

Christmas 1968   Not That He Brought Flowers

I am naturally pleased that the Poetry Book Society has made my book its Christmas choice. As this means that some eight hundred readers will receive a copy whether they want it or not, it is incumbent upon me to say something about these particular poems rather than about poetry in general.

I am a Welshman who has lived most of his life in Wales. I speak its language and know its problems, as well as its history and literature. These facts are responsible for some of the poems. As Welsh people form a very small proportion of the population of these islands, the appeal of such poems will be limited. A large majority of the people of the United Kingdom, Welsh or otherwise, is urban and participant in the scientific-technological revolution. Of what significance to them are the poetic statements of one who has deliberately kept to the backwaters of rural life, concerning himself with the things that are passing away? I am a priest of the Christian Church, another minority position, which will appear reactionary and functionless to most people. Yet all these facts about me have had some share in the production of the poems in this book.

I do not wish to isolate myself from my fellow poets. While each of us may be striving after some personal identity in his poetry, the difficulties of writing it are common to us all: the effort to marry the words and the tune; the struggle to keep the mind moving poetically; the concern to get right on paper what seemed right in the head; the task of avoiding propaganda, that is of exalting the message at the expense of the medium, or alternatively of perfecting the technique at the expense of the content.

Added to all this are the difficulties arising from the nature of contemporary society, transitional between the old one of the humanities and the new technological one. A poet is traditionally the custodian of language, as well as its renewer. In the age of the computer and the mass media, the proliferation of terms, the commercial inflation of adjectives, the encroachment of the novelist, can he still sustain his role? I do not wish to generalise a personal failure of talent. When the genius appears, he does easily what had seemed impossible. The poet of the new age may already have been hatched in some incubator or other. For myself I cannot boast even a guitar. I play on a small pipe, a little aside from the main road. But thank you for listening.   R. S. THOMAS

45

Summer 1969   Ingestion of Ice-Cream

The right place for writers of poems to appear, in relation to themselves as poem-writers, is in their poems.

Exegi monumentum is acceptable, if rash, in a poem.

Five paragraphs or one paragraph about oneself as confector of poems beginning *I believe, I do not wish, I write because, I am,* should be considered indecent and should be unacceptable.

Statements that *Poetry is, Poetry will become,* are presumptuous.

The pronouncements *I play in a mountain corner on a scrannel pipe* and *I play with myself in a confessional box without a curtain so that everyone can see the spasm on my face* are self-advertising equally.

No astrology, no playing witch or warlock.

Attaching to oneself a proletarian form of a Christian name is writing one's advertisement or wearing one's Order of Merit at an art auction of one's own pictures.

At a Poetry Festival or a writers' conference Coleridge and Hesiod are unlikely to be encountered.

Poetry, poem, – each word inclines to presumption, in relation to oneself. Even more so *poet.*

I regret a certain snobbery in these sentences.

I regret such relation as these sentences have or must have to the I myself of the poems which the selectors of the Poetry Book Society are so kindly recommending.

If I could concisely explain I myself or poems or my poems or writing them, I should try not to write them.

GEOFFREY GRIGSON

Autumn 1969   Terry Street

Yeats wrote in a letter of reply to a young woman who had sent him poems: '. . . one should love best what is nearest and most interwoven with one's life'. Although I have only just discovered this beautiful piece of advice in Hone's biography of Yeats, it is something that I think I have always known. Yeats was of course advising that girl to continue writing about her native Ireland, but with a Scotsman's effrontery and recklessness I choose to be blind to the real significance the advice should have for me. Scotland is what I most want to write about and what I am least able to. The only way I can try to describe the poetry I have written so far, and it is not really for me to do this, is to suggest that I have tried to understand the familiar and the ordinary.

This, I hope, is at least true of the poems I wrote in the second of the two years I lived in a terrace off Terry Street in Hull. It was never my intention that the poems be read as social or any other kind of protest, nor was I recommending Terry Street as a better because simpler way of life. My experience of the place made it impossible for me to want to do either of these things. The poems are not slum-pastorals.

Terry Street became for me a place of sad sanity. It was an alternative to the gaudy shams everywhere, a cave under a waterfall. But in thinking of Terry Street like this I was probably kidding myself into believing there could be a place not entirely of the age and yet handy enough to it for purposes of observation. Poverty makes men look foolish as well as their lives uncomfortable and I was no exception. I began to feel strange and lost, as though I was trying to inflict loneliness on myself, and I came to dislike Terry Street, and left it, although I still live in Hull. 'We free ourselves from obsession that we may be nothing. The last kiss is given to the void.'

DOUGLAS DUNN

Spring 1971   Moly

Picture Odysseus, deep in thought, walking through a dense green wood on a lonely island. He walks slowly but directly toward the house of the witch Circe, whom he has never seen. Yet he knows that she has turned his sailors into pigs, and he has no idea how he is going to rescue them or even save himself from the same transformation. Suddenly Hermes appears before him, in the guise of a boy – for a boy here helps the man. He tells Odysseus of the full difficulties before him and then shows him a herb growing at his feet, which he calls Moly. By eating this herb, Odysseus will be proof against Circe's powers.

It is magic, but if magic transforms us or keeps us proof against transformation, then it enters everybody's life. Magic is not completely separate from ordinary processes: it works by strengthening or inhibiting an impulse in us, even if that impulse is something we didn't recognize as being there. We can all take on the features of pigs – or what humans interpret as those features – we all have in us the germs of the brutal, greedy, and dull. And we can all avoid becoming pigs,

47

though to do so we must be wily and self-aware. Moly can help us to know our own potential for change: even though we are in the power of Circe or of time, we do not have to become pigs, we do not have to be unmanned, we are as free to make and unmake ourselves as we were at the age of ten.

Many a poet since Pound has liked to see himself as Odysseus, an explorer and adventurer who lives experience through, in detail, and yet can always extract himself from it. He is given to reflection, but as a moralist he is derivative. He is very lucky. He is aware of blood-powers and earth-powers that he does not fully understand, but they are sometimes very kind to him because he has recognized them and respected them. Their kindness most often takes the form of showing him the full range of possibilities when in a time of danger or despair there has seemed only one, and that a destructive one, available.

I am telling you how I see myself and how I see my book. It may be that this account of myself as a poet is only what I want to think. And there are certainly other ways of looking at my book. It could be seen as a debate between the passion for definition and the passion for flow, it could be seen as a history of San Francisco from 1965-9, or as a personal memoir of myself during those years. But I think of it as being about Odysseus' meeting with Hermes, his eating of that herb, and his reflections on metamorphosis in the remaining walk he has before he reaches the thick stone-built house.

THOM GUNN

Spring 1972   Celebrations

This book, which the Poetry Book Society has complimented me by choosing, is the work of a man approaching seventy. Such a man must have been formed and taught by persons mostly born in the mid-Victorian time, or even earlier. The social stratum into which I was born was gummed together by accepted ideas. There were occasional drop-outs (luckily there always are), but in general to vote Conserva-tive and go to church were automatic; social and sexual taboos sur-rounded one like barbed wire; and the arts were not much honoured.

Poetry, so far as it was thought of or 'taught' at all, mostly meant Virgil and Horace, Shakespeare, and *The Golden Treasury*. Boys were taught that verse must obey strict rules of metre, rhyme, and pro-priety. It is marvellous to have seen the abolition of such slavery, and a pleasure to agree with Nicanor Parra that *En poesiá se permite todo* – provided always, as he warns, that you improve on the blank page.

A boy of my destiny and temperament had to make his own escape-routes. For instance my destiny domiciled me, still adolescent, in South Africa, a country where my temperament made me recognize as enemies imperialism, nationalism, and apartheid. When, very early in life, I began, beneath the protective colouring of conformity, to lay fuses of subversiveness poets were my best teachers.

At fourteen, still at Rugby, I had found, unguided, *The Marriage of Heaven and Hell*. At seventeen, *The Symbolist Movement in Literature* sent me straight to Rimbaud. Born 1854, he was a contemporary of some of my kinsfolk and schoolmasters, but they would never have heard of him. Not that this made me or makes me despise them. It was not because they were unlovable or inhumane (with one exception) that I found their uniform of convention unwearable, but because (again with one exception) they showed no imagination.

'Are *all* your poems about people?' a questioner asked me after a poetry reading. Most of them are. Curiosity about human character and behaviour in particular times and places went to work, during my earlier years, in novels and short stories, occasional incursions into biography, and the editing of diaries. Later it found its focus more and more in verse. Not for me a sweeping denial or rejection of the past: it is present and alive to me, like the grandfather I knew (he comes into one of the poems in *Celebrations* and was born two years after Blake died). And not for me, I hope, alienation from the present, so full of charming and admirable characters of all ages.

When I was no more than eight years old, Ezra Pound was forecasting that 20th Century poetry would 'move against poppycock' and be 'harder and saner'. For himself, he wrote, he wanted it to be 'austere, direct, free from emotional slither'. Even in poetry there are always new kinds of poppycock to move against. In doing so, I have aimed at clarity and hope I have avoided 'emotional slither'.

WILLIAM PLOMER

Spring 1972   Some Time After

Nadezhda Mandelstam records a conversation with Boris Pasternak in which he distinguished between a 'book' and a 'collection' of poems, saying that only once did it happen to him to write a book. Certainly, poems written over a number of years are unlikely to have

49

the unity of inspiration implied in his definition, yet in so far as they reflect the 'fable' of an author's life – to use Edwin Muir's term – rather than its active surface, they must complement each other. The poems in *Some Time After* cover the last ten years or so of my life, a period in which I have also written drama, and have been interested in the problem of marrying words and music. They do not reflect the whole 'fable' of my life in that time, but as I re-read them I see that some themes recur, and that more poems than I was aware of are concerned with the mystery of human death.

Poetry is a way of discovering truth – this is one good reason for writing it; it is a discipline that helps one to face hard truths. The last poem in the book, written as a libretto, is an attempt to face the fact of death (whose bitterness is in parting from those we love) as something that has to be experienced fully, irrespective of any faith or lack of faith in immortality. Other poems are related to this, and the one quoted here, written about one of the superb concerts that Sir Thomas Beecham conducted at the very end of his life, sets two facts side by side: the blazing glory of his art and the darkness of extinction, two irreconcilable truths.

ANNE RIDLER

Autumn 1972   A Local Habitation

After the publication in 1954 of my third book of verse, *The Pot Geranium*, which, incidentally, was the first-ever Recommendation of the Poetry Book Society, I dried up as a poet. Until then my chief preoccupation had been with the Cumberland landscape seen as rock, with the little mining towns that came out of that rock, and with the dependence of even an urban and industrial society on the natural cycle of the seasons and the slower geological cycle of the rocks.

Then, one day, I began to think of my father and his family – of my grandmother, a game-keeper's daughter from Westmorland, who came to Millom in 1867, of her fourteen sons, of their many occupations and the part they played in the life of the town. And, almost without premeditation, I found myself writing *The Seventeenth of the Name*.

I began to turn over my memories of the last fifty years – of the old mines, the boreholes, the little locomotives, the Dole Days of the twenties, the schoolboy friends of that time – letting my memories grow up into the present just as the schoolboys have grown up in the houses and streets around me. I am still as concerned as ever with the problem of Man and his environment, but, in these poems, I write less about Man than about men – about my father, my uncles, friends and acquaintances from five generations in a small, self-contained and rather isolated community where you can hardly toss a penny into a crowd without hitting someone you are related to.

NORMAN NICHOLSON

Summer 1973   From Glasgow to Saturn

My writing has tended to penetrate a number of widely differing areas of experience rather than cultivate any one of them as central, though the Glasgow subject-matter seems to be what I most regularly return to. I was born in Glasgow and have lived most of my life there, and whatever image the city has to the outside world, to me it underlies and pervades my feeling at a deep level of identification and sympathy. At the moment it is in desperate throes of renewal, and some of the poems in this collection comment on the changes that are taking place.

Another group of poems is perhaps best described as science-fiction, though I would regard these as natural extensions of the imagination in an age of science. I do not share what is sometimes called the current disillusion with science and technology. I count myself lucky to have lived at a time of discoveries of such far-reaching potential as space travel must be. The poet, I think, is entitled to set up his camp on other worlds than this, and to bring back what he can in the way of human relevance.

The present volume opens with a fair number of short lyrics and songs, and I have found myself taking increasing pleasure from lyrical expression and from attempts to explore the strength of lightness. There are of course occasions when something very different is required, as in the 'Glasgow Sonnets', which asked for density and rigid form. But I have often been struck in recent years by the extraordinary resilience of the lyric mode, and I have no doubt that somewhere in the background are the achievements of popular song, whether pop or folk or their various admixtures, which in the last decade have blown the electric horns of elfland over poetry as well as life. I would certainly want to pay my tribute to the impact this music has had on me.

EDWIN MORGAN

51

Summer 1974
Twenty Years of the Poetry Book Society
(with lustral addendum i. m. James Reeves, 1909-1978)

New Zealand House, Haymarket. Sixteenth floor.
The city's white and greys and sudden green
Fill all the vista to the arching blue.

Cruelly level at this chopper's height,
The February sun. It shines on poets
Invited for an anniversary drink

And makes the party like the last in Proust.
To see bent veins, thin hair, large corporations,
Almost cheers one about one's own decay.

Dear co-slaves of the Muse, I might, if pressed
(The mid-day boozing clearly starts to work),
Approve your various poetries *en bloc*.

Such funny shapes to seek the beautiful,
Such feeble minds to make a cogent form,
Such egotists to interpret life and nature!

Are all we present mutual friends – or foes?
And does the rest of England, in the end,
Not require beauty, shape or explication?

Doubtless some fellow poets eyeing my
Trousers of daring check, plus clipped moustache
(With other curious traits that I don't see),

Are thereby confirmed in their low estimate
Of what I write – being less full of scotch
And sentiment and years than now I am.

I can't help thinking how in each crazed head
This narrow craftsmen's world is broadened out –
Beyond the urban concrete to the fields;

Into the empyrean; and the past.

52

*

That was the party, hearing a crash, I thought
Some awful bard (even a name occurred)
Was testing Martini's generosity

With over-zealousness. One later heard
Old purblind Reeves had blundered soberly
Among the empty glasses. We talked anon –

Strangely enough had never met before –
He kindly, and I'd always written well
(For once) of him. So on the cruel sea

Two rusty vessels passed. And now it's gone,
That power – to enchant the child and say
Neat forms – that wished to be immortal; may

Prove so, for in the end posterity
Seems to like quite as much as death and passion
Mild loves and mishaps in its forebears' art.

As they move clear of back-scratching and fashion,
Some even on Martini's sixteenth floor,
Share the few victories of the human heart.

ROY FULLER

Perhaps the first function of a poem is to assuage the poet's need for it to exist. For a while I found my needs satisfying themselves in images drawn from Anglo-Saxon kennings, Icelandic sagas, Viking excavations, and Danish and Irish bogs, and the result is the bulk of the poems in the first section of *North*. The second section is the result of a need to be explicit about pressures and prejudices watermarked into the psyche of anyone born and bred in Northern Ireland.

The title of the book, therefore, gestures towards the north of Ireland and the north of Europe. The first poems are set in Mossbawn, my earliest home, the last one in Wicklow, where I moved in 1972. Both place names have Norse elements. In fact, the language and landscape of Ireland, as the poem set on the archaeological site at Belderg insinuates, can be regarded as information retrieval systems for their own history: the bog bank is a memory bank.

The word 'bog' itself is one of the few borrowings in English from the Irish language. It means 'soft' in Irish, soft and wet, and one of its usages survives in the Hiberno-English expression, 'A soft day'. But in our part of the country we called the bog the 'moss', a word with Norse origins probably carried there by the Scots planters in the early seventeenth century. So in the bog/moss syndrome, one can diagnose a past of invasion, colonization and language shift, a past which, as Seamus Deane has pointed out, 'the Irish are conscious of as a process which is evidently unfulfilled'.

I cannot say why I should be possessed by past, language and landscape, but many of the poems wrought themselves out of that nexus; as Robert Frost put it, 'a poem begins as a lump in the throat, a homesickness, a lovesickness. It finds the thought and the thought finds the words'.

During the last few years there has been considerable expectation that poets from Northern Ireland should 'say' something about 'the situation', but in the end they will only be worth listening to if they are saying something about and to themselves. The truest poetry may be the most feigning but there are contexts, and Northern Ireland is one of them, where to feign a passion is as reprehensible as to feign its absence.

SEAMUS HEANEY

For some time I had felt that a lot of my poems had been tending towards the condition of fiction; presenting situations which might have been developed as short stories, containing characters whose full names and social backgrounds it seemed natural to give. Accordingly, in the autumn of 1973 I started on a novel, having what I considered were four important requisites for such an undertaking: a reasonable plot, a set of people I could put through all the hoops, a considerable didactic intention, and time.

The trouble was that ideas for poems still kept cropping up. As the novel was to offer a broad view of England in the 1970s, the poems were almost inevitably offshoots of the same enterprise. At first, they simply seemed to be about people who could not get into the novel. But as more and more of them nagged their way into the worksheets, it became clear to me that I wanted, or needed, to form them up into an extended sequence, closely interrelated in all its parts – just as we are interrelated in society. And that this sequence would be about the 'waste land' of our living at the present time.

The twelve poem-drafts on my table turned into twenty-two, the people in them ranging across the entire social scale from royalty to slum-dwellers. Walking round this array for four hours each morning over six weeks in the spring of 1974, filling out the character studies and the social detail, forging all the verbal links, was like playing a simultaneous chess match against twenty-two opponents. Looking up moves and tactics in the work of a score of modern English, American and European poets was a stimulus to continue rather than any help with the problems I had given myself. When the twenty-two poems were finished I took as an ironical title a phrase from *Twelfth Night* which I had been wanting to hitch onto a poem for years: the sequence became 'A Song of Good Life'.

In the midst of all this it was somehow possible, because the two tasks themselves linked up, to complete the play I had sketched out a year before. The alternatives offered by Feste in *Twelfth Night* when Sir Toby Belch asks for a song are 'a love song, or a song of good life'. So the play – which is no more about love in any finer sense than the poem-sequence is about genuine good living – became 'A Love Song'. The habit of irony is a bit difficult to drop.

These are the first two parts of the volume. The third comprises miscellaneous poems and jokes written between 1971 and 1974, and it seems odd to reflect that I had thought of this group as virtually a book in itself. Putting the three parts together made a volume roughly twice the length of any I had published before (satisfactorily out of the 'slim volume' syndrome, I thought) and I am grateful to my publishers and to the Poetry Book Society for their faith in it in these lean times...

ALAN BROWNJOHN

Christmas 1975   Driving West

The title poem of this volume, 'Driving West', which occurs halfway through the book, is pivotal rather than central. The journey it describes – from London to Devon – was a real one certainly but the poem is also to an extent allegorical. My present home in Devon is a few miles away from where I was born and brought up and though for the first twenty years of my adult life I cared very little for the place and indeed hardly ever went there, in middle age I have become increasingly involved with it. This means of course that I write more about it, that I write with greater intensity when I'm there and, I think, differently in general.

It is often said that one of the leading characteristics of the Georgian poets was to live in one place and long to be in another. There are far worse characteristics that a poet could display, but I don't think the comment quite applies to myself and my work, principally because though, for family reasons, I live mostly in London, and frequently long to be in Devon, it's not fruitless longing; I do in fact spend a great deal of time there. The Devon house has certainly influenced my work. It is situated in a busy agricultural valley where nothing has been artificially preserved or beautified and where very few tourists come.

I have tried to describe the landscape in such poems as 'Frost on the Shortest Day', 'Mist in the Otter Valley' and in the set of self-contained, haiku-type verses – one for each month – 'January to December'. I have also written about the happenings of the place, often apparently trivial incidents of the present which have given significance to events and feelings of three decades ago, as in 'The Landgirl at the Boss's Grave'.

The first half of the book consists of heterogeneous themes that are neither urban nor rural, except one that is both, that is, urban in subject matter, rural in metaphor. This poem, 'Noises from the School,' in fact first alerted me as to where my area of greatest poetic

56

concentration was, for the time being at least, to lie. Themes of childhood, first released by the writing of an autobiography seven years ago, still recur ('Called Home', for example), reshaped by adult experience.

Increasingly I get impetus from being commissioned to write on a particular subject. The ingenuity needed initially to discover some aspect of the set theme which genuinely involves one poetically is a stimulus to the imagination. Greatly as I revere Milton I could not at first write a poem for his Festival but when I concentrated on my father's admiration of his work, I could go forward with zest; 'John Milton and my Father.'

PATRICIA BEER

Spring 1976   Behind the Eyes (Collected Poems)

The earliest of my poems to be printed were written at the end of World War One, in which I served in the infantry. It was a time never free from conflict or stress, and the pastoral calm which seems to haunt the self-expression of the writer is a transient gift. I am grateful to the Poetry Book Society for giving me the opportunity of saying a few words on the make-up of my Collected Poems which is recommended in the bulletin. The Collected Poems is not a simple re-print of the volume so named published in 1947 (and long since out of print). It gives a wider choice from my poems to that date, and is extended to include new pieces which have accrued in the intervening period.

The appearance of a new edition of my Collected Poems is the result of a chance meeting with a poet – a poet who doubled as poet and publisher, and was one of those inexplicable generosities of the God of Chance. A lot of the poems have undergone textual revision. The first poems to be printed, in 1919, form a small group whose derivation was war experience 1917-18. These, I think, show that one had shaken off the trammels of one's early masters, though in the transition from war experience to the peace confusion which followed, there were some reversions to the earlier and romantic stylisms. Most of this, the fresh and the jaded, were swept into one of those slender first volumes which fire the aspiring author's ambitions higher. I have included about half the contents of this first volume here. Of course at that age, with one's foot on the first rung of the ladder, anything or everything seems possible. The choice, in fact, never presented itself.

The influence of Rimbaud tempted me to a Messianic role which I could not fulfill, and I had to be content with the role of a looker-on. Most of my second volume *Invocation to Angels* was written in this mood.

The third slim volume *Twittingpan* and some others (also reprinted entire), sharply exchanges the role of looker-on for that of voyeur. The decor and the puppets are no longer regarded with aesthetic or philosophical detachment, they are subjected to a satirical bastinado. For ten years one had looked to poetry for an answer. This was never forthcoming. Some of the later and longer poems in *Invocation* have a distinct inclination towards nihilism, a tendency which I did not wish to develop, but countered with a turn towards sarcasm and satire. My satire was directed at manners not morals, at attitudes not persons, not at the holder of the office. This sort of preoccupation led to a closer observation of the political ambience and was no doubt the sense of a need to have a more direct influence on the social environment. Strange that one should give up writing verse just as one's juniors were bringing about a successful revival of it. One exception there was in my case, an attack on the statesman most closely identified with the hypocritical Non-Intervention agreement, which emerged as the poem entitled 'to the wife of a Non-Interventionist statesman' – written during the time of the Spanish civil war, a period which undoubtedly influenced many of the writers of the day, and which became the 'Cause' of the '30's. Also in the 1930's Magus and Beatnik were able to speak on equal terms.

EDGELL RICKWORD

Christmas 1976   The Dream-House

It is quite a long time, perhaps almost a year, since I wrote a poem. This kind of drought fills some writers with terror, even if they have experienced it before. I feel, rather, regret at the absence of something I once cared desperately about, the loss of a dimension of perception and action (like remembering the urgency of being in love) and I cast around fitfully, half-expecting the shock of a sudden bite.

There are ways back, I think: for different poets different ways. I believe in application, regularity, discipline; working long hours for a publisher during the last few years, I have failed to measure up to my standards. It is important (for me) to treat writing poetry as a practising Christian treats prayer: to get on with it, to be available for grace.

Secondly, I know there are a number of places that have often fired me – the demanding North Norfolk marshland, certain hill forts, ruins. To return to them excites my imagination: the first poem in *The Dream-House*, 'Hills', was written after going back to the land of my childhood in the Chilterns, and it ended a drought.

Two main preoccupations recur in these poems. One is a keen interest in relating past to present. Poems like 'In the Company of Saints', 'At Mycenae', 'History' and 'Fortification' are really cele-brations of continuity. Whether I am noting how little the unspec-tacular lives of Greek shepherds change through centuries, or how a kite-flier almost unthinkingly perpetuates a ritual, describing how a Celtic church half-buried in sand still permeates peace, or stripping skins from a familiar landscape and imagining it as it used to be, I am simply suggesting that the past is a great force at our disposal if we have the wits to make use of it. We are 'hosts to the living dead' and can barely afford to turn our backs on so much experience.

The other preoccupation is with destiny. It seems true that there are certain tides from which we cannot escape and yet (as in the business of writing poetry) we can to some extent fashion our own fate. Poems like 'The Dream-House' which describes a wake, and 'A Little Faith at Brattahlid' which was the last Viking settlement in Green-land, try to explore attitudes – stoic and stubborn – to destiny. And it seemed appropriate, in this connexion, to include a translation of the fine but very little-known Anglo-Saxon poem, 'The Fates of Men'.

This collection also includes a number of riddles with which I've had much fun at poetry readings: the clues range through history, folklore, current affairs, literature and language, and the answers are all Christian names.

It remains to say that I am proud and grateful that *The Dream-House* has been chosen by the Poetry Book Society and that I do hope you enjoy it.

KEVIN CROSSLEY-HOLLAND

In an introduction to my first pamphlet collection, *The Small Containers*, I wrote that poetry was, for me, concerned with knowing and understanding. This conviction has deepened: I would like my poems to be windows, not mirrors. A window frames a scene which has its own strong and independent life; the personality of the poet both shapes that scene and is subordinate to it. The frame, however, is important. A window cuts a shape, and I am fascinated by structure, harmony, balance – all those qualities which give definition to the view which the window elects to show.

I am writing in a room where the most disparate objects, an Etruscan bronze, a grey felt mouse, a microscope, a sixteenth century bible, live in a chosen harmony. They are, if you like, substantial images: metaphors drawn together in a relationship which compels my affection. The room contains the centuries, and I feel acutely ill-at-ease in places where *now* is the only dimension visible; life is a texture where past and present become each other. In my poems I have tried to feel my way into worlds where the dead dance their measures with the living, and the eye is pleased by the easy communion which they share.

In *Prehistories*, my last book, a recurrent theme was our bond, strong though half-understood, with the stones and silences of periods before recorded history. All images came together in the sight of my children huddled against the wind under the stone burial-chamber of a long barrow, my wife carrying an unborn child and 'Poised on Chun Quoit into the flying sky'. In this new book, *The Hinterland*, I have drawn my images from that great shadow-land of Western making and doing which, over the last couple of thousand years, has shaped and is shaping all that we are. Voices speak to our condition from the cast of a girl, asphyxiated in her flight from Pompeii, the margins of the leaf of a mediaeval manuscript, the scrawled recipes of a farmer in his rubbed almanac.

The centrepiece of the book is a sequence of fifteen linked sonnets, written in a state of absorbed puzzlement over four or five days: one of those occasions rare, but compelling gratitude. Images from the sequence had teased me for years, but I had ploughed them under, knowing I had no proper home for them. The sequence moves backwards and forwards from the years 1914-1918, a meditation on complexities of creation and destruction.

I hope that in these poems, though search begins in clouds and in enigmas, the world becomes clear, accurate and substantial. Rilke's dictum is a good one to end with: 'He was a poet and hated the approximate'.

PETER SCUPHAM

Spring 1978   The Cost of Seriousness

A writer finds some of his works more difficult to introduce than others, and as I have had poems chosen by the Poetry Book Society before, I trust that subscribers will excuse my offering a shorter-than-usual prefatory piece. Perhaps I should try to explain the title. I chose it (it is a poem title also, of course,) because it seemed to me to describe the book's main concern, which is with the inability of art (poetry in this case) to alter human circumstances or alleviate human distress. I think such a point needs making in an age when we are being urged to produce ever more urgent and extreme forms of art. After Auschwitz, they say, all art must be existential and at the edge of desperation. I am sure that the opposite is the case. It is the duty of art to make palatable somehow the real tragedy of the world. It must tell the truth about the facts of that tragedy at the same time. This is a tall order but one which poets have to face up to. One way of doing so, I believe, is to question the machinery of language, to try to test the worth of the words we use to describe our feelings. I don't mean games with words but a constant awareness of the shapes language makes of itself. Such questioning means that poetry can never hope to be very popular. Yet its feelings should be universal.

To come to the particular: most of the poems in this book were written after the sudden and tragic death of my wife at the end of 1974. The grief is personal, but I hope the poems communicate to other people, and say something more than just regret. Those about my wife – *An Angel in Blythburgh Church, An Exequy, The Delegate, The Easiest Room in Hell* and *Evensong* share the centre of the book with the *Three Transportations,* attempts to settle the empty continent of Australia with notable examples of the European and the American imaginations. The frame around them is made of poems about England, Australia and the arts of literature, music and painting. There is an attempt at the end to look forward to a renewal of life. The title poem asks whether our emotions can be notated properly in words, and the poem about the Renaissance painter Melozzo da Forli

61

asserts (but not too sadly) that art is 'only a language of gestures'. But the shape of the gestures counts, and I hope some of the shapes in my book make sense to their readers, and look as if they'll last a while.

PETER PORTER

Summer 1978 Paradise Illustrated

Several years ago I was compiling a Choice of Milton's Verse, and during the preparatory reading it struck me with fresh force that in *Paradise Lost,* for all his grandness of gesture, Milton had managed quite nimbly, if not to explain *why* we are as we are, then at least to describe *how* we are. Whether the presumed cause – disobeying God in respect of an apple – is a fiction or not, the account of the effects is true enough.

Out of that mountainous reading *(parturiunt montes . . .)* came the title-sequence of the present book, which aims to illustrate in fairly homely terms the course of events between Adam's naming of the animals and the death of Eve, and to glance sidelong at some of the repercussions – not all of them wholly regrettable – of our fall from grace. There were moments when only Milton's words would do, but the poems here are in none but the most blatant sense 'Miltonic'. Indeed, at times they approach the mode of the comic strip – though their treatment of these primal matters is not, I hope, entirely flippant. The flashforwards or 'anachronistic' references to more recent developments – the one little bonus still available – are certainly not meant as mockery, but rather as a tribute to the perpetual interest of the story of Adam and Eve. That Eve has the last word has nothing to do with her being 'a woman', but much to do with her being closer to us: she seems to have been created 'fallen', or not far from it, whereas Adam is very conscious (as few of us can be) of his place as the first of his sort and the right-hand man of the Almighty.

It was Milton who remarked, in a different connection, that he could not praise a cloistered virtue, unexercised and unbreathed, and even he found difficulty in representing a state of perfect innocence, however fleetingly. Many writers, Christian or otherwise, have depicted the evils resulting from the loss of innocence, and so I have tried to indicate what was gained, too, or can be – or perhaps simply to suggest that, despite all that can be said against the human condition, it is the only one we have.

The miscellaneous poems which complete the collection are some of them obviously hangovers from Eden. 'The words were all before them, which to choose . . .' However miscellaneous in subject or tone, it would be surprising did they not relate somehow or other to that equivocal breed which 'our general mother' initiated when she bit into the apple.

It remains for me to thank the Poetry Book Society for choosing this volume and to hope that members will find something to enjoy – or at any rate to recognize – therein.   D. J. Enright

---

Summer 1978   Selected Poems 1951–1974

In putting together a selected poems that spans well over twenty years of writing, one re-experiences to a certain extent some of the tensions that went into the making of the various collections. Perhaps even more acutely there comes back to the mind the challenge of those moments – or rather months, and sometimes years – of transition between one book and another. Factors that made the transitions possible, fears and silences that threatened them – these are the presences that rise up once more.

I have tried in assembling this choice of my work to include those pieces which for me were essential to this process of poetic growth. Thus, though I was willing to sacrifice virtually the whole of my first pamphlet, *Relations and Contraries* of 1951, it contained a poem, 'Wakening with the Window over Fields', written in 1948, which I kept. This was the first poem of mine where I seemed to hear a world beyond myself that defined its existence in terms of a syncopated melody (thus pulling away from traditional metric) and also in terms of space, light and air. I knew now what I wanted to do, though I did not know how to do it.

In those days the air waves seemed to be filled with the voice of Dylan Thomas, and the problem for a young poet – at least for *this* young poet – was to get beyond it towards something a little less lush. A step in this direction was made possible by the discovery of those poems of Wallace Stevens like 'Thirteen Ways of Looking at a Blackbird' – poems written in discrete fragments that permitted you to be true to immediate sensations without transforming them into grand opera. A little book, *The Necklace* of 1955, got me from 'Wakening with the Window over Fields' to its final poem, 'Fiascherino', where the fragments of sensation seemed to knit up into a more organic whole.

This new unity came about because I had started to consider syntax, and it was precisely this – meditating the relation between the shapes of sentences and the way we perceive things – that broadened the style invented in *The Necklace* and helped me write my first full-scale book, *Seeing is Believing* (1960).

It is not my intention here to map an entire poetic progress, but to point out one or two saliences. Often a poem proves to be more of a bridge than one could have imagined at the time of its composition. From *The Way of a World* (1969) I began writing poems about politics and history – in *The Shaft* (1978), a recent PBS recommendation, there is, for instance, a sequence of poems about the French Revolution. I have retained in my *Selected Poems* a piece conceived when I was writing *The Necklace* in Italy in 1952, though not actually written until the early 60's. This poem, which appeared in *A Peopled Landscape* (1963), is called 'Up at La Serra'. As a poem, it is not perhaps entirely mature, but it represents my first attempt to grapple with a situation in which history has closed off alternatives and brought the protagonist to a pitch of crisis. Written so long ago, it seems to underlie many more recent poems such as 'Charlotte Corday' and 'For Danton' in *The Shaft* and, in the present selection, 'Prometheus', 'Assassin' and, in a rather different way, 'At Stoke'. But I must leave the reader to trace these continuities for himself, and trust that they are evidence not merely of personal concerns, but of general human ones.

CHARLES TOMLINSON

Autumn 1978   Tenebrae

Tenebrae is my fourth volume of poetry and appears seven years after the previous collection, *Mercian Hymns,* which was a Poetry Book Society Choice in 1971. It may be, in some respects, a reaction against that earlier work which was a sequence of 'hymns' written in rhythmic prose. The dominant form in this new collection is the sonnet. In other respects, though, there is continuity. *Tenebrae* shares with *Mercian Hymns* and, indeed, with my first and second books, *For the Unfallen* and *King Log,* a sense of history (neither 'Whig' nor Marxist) and a sense of place (neither topographical nor anecdotal). Many of the poems in *Tenebrae* are concerned with the strange likeness and ultimate unlikeness of sacred and profane love; and it is this concern which, perhaps, creates the dominant tone of the book.

Although a poet must put a great deal of himself into his work I have never been able to agree with those who say that poetry is 'self-expression'. When I was twenty I thought that Eliot, at the end of the second section of 'Tradition and the Individual Talent' was absolutely right; and at forty-six, having been taught to be broad-minded and wary, I still think that he was more right than wrong.

GEOFFREY HILL

Poetry Book Society
Choices and Recommendations (R) 1954-78

1954   SPRING   Vernon Watkins   *The Death Bell*   Faber
                              Norman Nicholson   *The Pot Geranium*   Faber (R)
        SUMMER   George Barker   *A Vision of Beasts and Gods*   Faber
        AUTUMN   Frances Cornford   *Collected Poems*   Cresset
        CHRISTMAS   Sheila Wingfield   *A Kite's Dinner*   Cresset

1955   SPRING   Laurie Lee   *My Many-Coated Man*   Deutsch
                              Norman MacCaig   *Riding Lights*   Hogarth (R)
        SUMMER   Lawrence Durrell   *The Tree of Idleness*   Faber
                              William Plomer   *A Shot in the Park*   Cape (R)
        AUTUMN   Robin Skelton   *Patmos*   R.K.P.
                              Dorothy Wellesley   *Early Light*   Hart-Davis (R)
        CHRISTMAS   Herbert Read   *Moon's Farm*   Faber
                              Elizabeth Jennings   *A Way of Looking*   Deutsch (R)
                              G. J. Warnock   *Poems*   Blackwell (R)

1956   SPRING   Edwin Muir   *One Foot in Eden*   Faber
                              E. J. Scovell   *The River Steamer*   Cresset (R)
        SUMMER   New Poems 1956   *Ed S. Spender, E. Jennings & D. Abse*
                                                                Michael Joseph
        AUTUMN   W. S. Merwin   *Green with Beasts*   Hart-Davis
                              Kathleen Nott   *Poems from the North*   Hand & Flower (R)
        CHRISTMAS   John Holloway   *The Minute*   Marvell
                              Kingsley Amis   *A Case of Samples*   Gollancz (R)
                              Siegfried Sassoon   *Sequences*   Faber (R)

1957   SPRING   C. A. Trypanis   *The Stones of Troy*   Faber
                              Norman Cameron   *Collected Poems*   Hogarth (R)
                              Burns Singer   *Still and All*   Secker (R)
        SUMMER   Louis MacNeice   *Visitations*   Faber
                              Edmund Blunden   *Poems of Many Years*   Collins (R)
                              Thom Gunn   *The Sense of Movement*   Faber (R)
        AUTUMN   Ted Hughes   *The Hawk in the Rain*   Faber
                              Roy Campbell   *Collected Poems, Volume 2*   Bodley Head (R)
        CHRISTMAS   Theodore Roethke   *Words for the Wind*   Secker
                              Randolph Stow   *Act One*   Macdonald (R)

1958   SPRING   Thomas Kinsella   *Another September*   Dolmen: O.U.P.
                              Michael Hamburger   *The Dual Site*   R.K.P. (R)
        SUMMER   John Smith   *Excursus in Autumn*   Hutchinson
                              Patrick MacDonogh   *One Landscape Still*   Secker (R)
        AUTUMN   A. S. J. Tessimond   *Selection*   Putnam
                              R. S. Thomas   *Poetry for Supper*   Hart-Davis (R)
        CHRISTMAS   New Poems 1958   *Ed B. Dobree, L. MacNeice & P. Larkin*
                                                          Michael Joseph
                              James K. Baxter   *In Fires of no Return*   O.U.P. (R)

1959   SPRING   Patricia Beer   *Loss of the Magyar*   Longmans
                              Laurence Lerner   *Domestic Interior*   Hutchinson (R)

1959	SUMMER	Guinness Book of Poetry 1957/58 Putnam
		P. J. Kavanagh *One and One* Heinemann (R)
		Christopher Logue *Songs* Hutchinson (R)
	AUTUMN	Donald Davie *The Forests of Lithuania* Marvell

1960	SPRING	Peter Levi *The Gravel Ponds* Deutsch
	SUMMER	Patrick Kavanagh *Come Dance with Kitty Stobling* Longmans
		William Plomer *Collected Poems* Cape (R)
		James Reeves *Collected Poems 1929-1959* Heinemann (R)
	AUTUMN	Dom Moraes *Poems* Eyre & S.
	CHRISTMAS	John Betjeman *Summoned by Bells* Murray

1961	SPRING	David Holbrook *Imaginings* Putman
		Louis MacNeice *Solstices* Faber (R)
	SUMMER	Elizabeth Jennings *Song for a Birth or a Death* Deutsch
		John Wain *Weep Before God* Macmillan (R)
	AUTUMN	R. S. Thomas *Tares* Hart-Davis
		Thomas Blackburn *A Smell of Burning* Putnam (R)
		Alan Brownjohn *The Railings* Digby (R)
		Edward Lucie-Smith *A Tropical Childhood* O.U.P. (R)
	CHRISTMAS	Peter Redgrove *The Nature of Cold Weather* R.K.P.
		Richard Kell *Control Tower* Chatto (R)
		Jon Silkin *The Re-Ordering of the Stones* Chatto (R)

1962	SPRING	Patrick Creagh *A Row of Pharaohs* Heinemann
		George Barker *The View from a Blind I* Faber (R)
	SUMMER	Dannie Abse *Poems, Golders Green* Hutchinson
		Vernon Scannell *A Sense of Danger* Putnam (R)
	AUTUMN	Thomas Kinsella *Downstream* Dolmen : O.U.P.
		Roy Fuller *Collected Poems* Deutsch (R)
	CHRISTMAS	Michael Baldwin *Death on a Live Wire* Longmans
		Robert Graves *New Poems 1962* Cassell (R)

1963	SPRING	Richard Murphy *Sailing to an Island* Faber
		George MacBeth *The Broken Places* Scorpion (R)
		Rosemary Tonks *Notes on Cafes and Bedrooms* Putnam (R)
	SUMMER	Alexander Baird *Poems* Chatto
		Bernard Spencer *With Luck Lasting* Hodder (R)
		Charles Tomlinson *A Peopled Landscape* O.U.P. (R)
	AUTUMN	Louis MacNeice *The Burning Perch* Faber
		Austin Clarke *Flight to Africa* Dolmen : O.U.P. (R)
	CHRISTMAS	Patricia Beer *The Survivors* Longmans
		Geoffrey Grigson *Collected Poems 1924-1961* Phoenix (R)
		Brian Higgins *Notes While Travelling* Longmans (R)

1964	SPRING	Philip Larkin *The Whitsun Weddings* Faber
	SUMMER	Donald Davie *Events and Wisdoms* R.K.P.
		Thomas Blackburn *A Breathing Space* Putnam (R)
	AUTUMN	C. A. Trypanis *Pompeian Dog* Faber
		James Reeves *The Questioning Tiger* Heinemann (R)
		Anne Sexton *Selected Poems* O.U.P. (R)
	CHRISTMAS	Patric Dickinson *This Cold Universe* Chatto
		Edward Lucie-Smith *Confessions and Histories* O.U.P. (R)
		Frank Prewett *Collected Poems* Cassell (R)

1965	SPRING	Sylvia Plath *Ariel* Faber
		David Gascoyne *Collected Poems* O.U.P. (R)
		Norman MacCaig *Measures* Chatto (R)
		David Wright *Adam at Evening* Hodder (R)
	SUMMER	Roy Fuller *Buff* Deutsch
		D. J. Enright *The Old Adam* Chatto (R)
		George MacBeth *A Doomsday Book* Scorpion (R)
		George Barker **The True Confession* MacGibbon
		*Special Commendation
	AUTUMN	John Holloway *Wood and Windfall* R.K.P.
		Paul Dehn *Fern on the Rock* Hamilton (R)
		John Heath-Stubbs *Selected Poems* O.U.P. (R)
		John Smith *A Discreet Immorality* Hart-Davis (R)
	CHRISTMAS	Kathleen Raine *The Hollow Hill* Hamilton
		C. Day Lewis *The Room* Cape (R)
		Christopher Middleton *Nonsequences* Longmans (R)

1966	SPRING	Charles Tomlinson *American Scenes* O.U.P.
		Ruth Pitter *Still by Choice* Cresset (R)
		A. K. Ramanujan *The Striders* O.U.P. (R)
	SUMMER	Brian Higgins *The Northern Fiddler* Methuen
		Anne Halley *Between Wars* O.U.P. (R)
	AUTUMN	Norman MacCaig *Surroundings* Chatto
		James K. Baxter *Pig Island Letters* O.U.P. (R)
	CHRISTMAS	Peter Redgrove *The Force* R.K.P.
		Edward Brathwaite *Rights of Passage* O.U.P. (R)
		Louis Zukofsky *'A' 1-12* Cape (R)

1967	SPRING	Austin Clarke *Old-Fashioned Pilgrimage* Dolmen: O.U.P.
	SUMMER	John Fuller *The Tree that Walked* Chatto
		Geoffrey Grigson *A Skull in Salop* Macmillan (R)
	AUTUMN	Thom Gunn *Touch* Faber
		Elizabeth Jennings *Collected Poems* Macmillan (R)
	CHRISTMAS	Anthony Hecht *The Hard Hours* O.U.P.
		Thomas Kinsella *Nightwalker* Dolmen (R)

1968	SPRING	Charles Causley *Underneath the Water* Macmillan
		Tony Connor *Kon in Springtime* O.U.P. (R)
	SUMMER	Roy Fuller *New Poems* Deutsch
		Austin Clarke *The Echo at Coole* Dolmen (R)
	AUTUMN	Derek Mahon *Night-Crossing* O.U.P.
		Geoffrey Hill *King Log* Deutsch (R)
		Richard Murphy *The Battle of Aughrim* Faber (R)
	CHRISTMAS	R. S. Thomas *Not that he Brought Flowers* Hart-Davis
		Barry Cole *Moonsearch* Methuen (R)

1969	SPRING	Peter Whigham *The Blue Winged Bee* Anvil
	SUMMER	Seamus Heaney *Door into the Dark* Faber
		Geoffrey Grigson *Ingestion of Ice-Cream* Macmillan (R)
		David Harsent *A Violent Country* O.U.P. (R)
	AUTUMN	Douglas Dunn *Terry Street* Faber
	CHRISTMAS	David Holbrook *Old World, New World* Rapp & Whiting

1970	SPRING	W. S. Graham *Malcolm Mooney's Land* Faber
	SUMMER	Ian Hamilton *The Visit* Faber
		Glyn Hughes *Neighbours* Macmillan (R)
		Hugo Williams *Sugar Daddy* O.U.P. (R)
	AUTUMN	Peter Porter *The Last of England* O.U.P.
		John Montague *Tides* Dolmen (R)
	CHRISTMAS	Elizabeth Jennings *Lucidities* Macmillan
1971	SPRING	Thom Gunn *Moly* Faber
		Roy Fisher *Matrix* Fulcrum (R)
		Jon Silkin *Amana Grass* Chatto (R)
	SUMMER	Geoffrey Hill *Mercian Hymns* Deutsch
		John Cotton *Old Movies* Chatto (R)
		Kathleen Raine *The Lost Country* Dolmen: Hamilton (R)
	AUTUMN	Sylvia Plath *Winter Trees* Faber
	CHRISTMAS	Gavin Ewart *The Gavin Ewart Show* Trigram
		Molly Holden *Air and Chill Earth* Chatto (R)
		X. J. Kennedy *Breaking and Entering* O.U.P. (R)
		W. R. Rodgers *Collected Poems* O.U.P. (R)
1972	SPRING	William Plomer *Celebrations* Cape
		Anne Ridler *Some Time After* Faber (R)
	SUMMER	D. J. Enright *Daughters of Earth* Chatto
		Alan Brownjohn *Warrior's Career* Macmillan (R)
	AUTUMN	Norman Nicholson *A Local Habitation* Faber
		Iain Crichton Smith *Love Poems and Elegies* Gollancz (R)
	CHRISTMAS	Stewart Conn *An Ear to the Ground* Hutchinson
		Wayne Brown *On The Coast* Deutsch (R)
		Charles Tomlinson *Written on Water* O.U.P. (R)
1973	SPRING	John Smith *Entering Rooms* Chatto
		Norman MacCaig *The White Bird* Chatto (R)
	SUMMER	Edwin Morgan *From Glasgow to Saturn* Carcanet
		J. C. Hall *A House of Voices* Chatto (R)
		James K. Baxter *Runes* O.U.P. (R)
		Lawrence Durrell *Vega* Faber (R)
	AUTUMN	Michael Burn *Out on a Limb* Chatto
	CHRISTMAS	Alasdair Maclean *From the Wilderness* Gollancz
1974	SPRING	Geoffrey Holloway *Rhine Jump* London Magazine
		Jon Stallworthy *Hand in Hand* Chatto (R)
	AUTUMN	Douglas Dunn *Love or Nothing* Faber
		Charles Tomlinson *The Way In* O.U.P.
		Brian Jones *For Mad Mary* London Magazine (R)
		George Kendrick *Bicycle Tyre in a Tall Tree* Carcanet (R)
	CHRISTMAS	Andrew Waterman *Living Room* Marvell
1975	SPRING	John Cotton *Kilroy Was Here* Chatto
		Iain Crichton Smith *The Notebooks of Robinson Crusoe* Gollancz (R)
	SUMMER	Seamus Heaney *North* Faber
		Roy Fuller *From the Joke Shop* Deutsch (R)

1975	AUTUMN	Peter Porter *Living in a Calm Country* O.U.P.
		Alan Brownjohn *A Song of Good Life* Secker (R)
		D. J. Enright *Sad Ires and Others* Chatto (R)
	CHRISTMAS	Vernon Scannell *The Loving Game* Robson
		Patricia Beer *Driving West* Gollancz (R)
		John Montague *A Slow Dance* Dolmen (R)

1976	SPRING	George Barker *Dialogues Etc* Faber
		Peter Reading *The Prison Cell & Barrel Mystery* Secker (R)
		Edgell Rickword *Behind the Eyes (Collected Poems)*
		Carcanet (R)
	SUMMER	Hugh Maxton *The Noise of the Fields* Dolmen
		Jim Burns *The Goldfish Speaks from Beyond the Grave*
		Salamander (R)
		Harry Guest *A House Against the Night* Anvil (R)
	AUTUMN	Thom Gunn *Jack Straw's Castle* Faber
		Peter Bland *Mr. Maui* London Magazine (R)
	CHRISTMAS	Kevin Crossley-Holland *The Dream-House* Deutsch
		John Hewitt *Time Enough* Blackstaff (R)
		John Pudney *Living in a One-Sided House*
		Shepheard-Walwyn (R)

1977	SPRING	Tom Paulin *A State of Justice* Faber
		Peter Scupham *The Hinterland* O.U.P. (R)
	SUMMER	Michael Hamburger *Real Estate* Carcanet
		Peter Redgrove *From Every Chink of the Ark* R.K.P. (R)
		Anthony Thwaite *A Portion for Foxes* O.U.P. (R)
	AUTUMN	W. S. Graham *Implements in Their Places* Faber
		Donald Davie *In the Stopping Train* Carcanet (R)
	CHRISTMAS	Frank Ormsby *A Store of Candles* O.U.P.
		Kit Wright *The Bear Looked over the Mountain*
		Salamander (R)

1978	SPRING	Peter Porter *The Cost of Seriousness* O.U.P.
		Charles Tomlinson *The Shaft* O.U.P. (R)
		Jeffrey Wainwright *Heart's Desire* Carcanet (R)
	SUMMER	D. J. Enright *Paradise Illustrated* Chatto
		James Simmons *The Selected James Simmons* Blackstaff (R)
		Charles Tomlinson *Selected Poems 1951-1974* O.U.P. (R)
	AUTUMN	Geoffrey Hill *Tenebrae* Deutsch
		Geoffrey Grigson *The Fiesta* Secker (R)
		Ted Walker *Burning the Ivy* Cape (R)
	CHRISTMAS	Roy Fisher *The Thing About Joe Sullivan* Carcanet
		Wes Magee *No Man's Land* Blackstaff (R)
		John Hewitt *The Rain Dance* Blackstaff (R)

Selectors of Choices
1954-78

Dannie Abse
J. R. Ackerley
W. H. Auden
Patricia Beer
Thomas Blackburn
Alan Brownjohn
Nevill Coghill
Cyril Connolly
Patric Dickinson
Martin Dodsworth
Douglas Dunn
T. F. Eagleton
Colin Falck

Ian Fletcher
G. S. Fraser
John Fuller
Roy Fuller
J. C. Hall
Michael Hamburger
Ian Hamilton
Christopher Hassall
John Hayward
John Holloway
Ted Hughes
Frank Kermode
Philip Larkin

Naomi Lewis
Karl Miller
Stuart Montgomery
Edwin Muir
Gabriel Pearson
James Reeves
V. Sackville-West
Janet Adam Smith
Anthony Thwaite
Terence Tiller
Vernon Watkins
David Wright

Printed by the John Roberts Press, London
for the Poetry Book Society
105 Piccadilly, London WIV OAU